ON READING SHAKESPEARE

ON
Reading Shakespeare

BY

LOGAN PEARSALL SMITH

HARCOURT, BRACE AND COMPANY

NEW YORK

Fourth printing, August, 1935

PRINTED IN THE UNITED STATES OF AMERICA

BY QUINN & BODEN COMPANY, INC., RAHWAY, N. J.

Typography by Robert S. Josephy

CONTENTS

ON NOT READING SHAKESPEARE

Chapter I

ON NOT READING SHAKESPEARE

I AM NOT a Shakespeare scholar, nor am I a constant reader of his plays. I cannot say with Coleridge that no day of my life had passed without opening one or another of those volumes. I have, of course, read and re-read Shakespeare—there have been times in my life when this has been one of my main occupations. But intervals have often elapsed between these perusals; sometimes long intervals, when I haven't, it is true, forgotten Shakespeare—one cannot do that—but when a kind of resentment, a touch of exasperation, has kept my thoughts from the subject.

The truth is that the world's great writers are apt to become the world's great bores. We must put on our finest moods for their society, and these court-costumes of the soul are not comfortable for long. And then the Masters ask—or their admirers ask on their behalf—for more attention than we have time to give them. Homer, Virgil, Dante, Shakespeare—a whole life of study can be well devoted to each of these; and fate has vouchsafed us only one brief span of distracted existence. There is always the risk, too, that what begins as a taste may become an obsession. The works of great writers doze with their backs to us on our shelves for years, but they are dangerous company. Potent spirits lie impris-

3

oned in those leather bottles. The names inscribed upon them are names which have defeated time, and may exert a formidable spell on us. Opening a volume of this kind in an idle moment, we may be seized upon, be-jinned and captured. We want only to look up a quotation perhaps in some old author, but we must go on, page after page, and then go on to read all the books we can find about him. The reader becomes a student, the student a bigot, and what is justly called a blind admirer, for his eyes are blinded by gazing on the object of his worship. Blemishes and merits are all blurred together, and faults seem to him perfections. Such a specialist is the last person in the world to give a measured and rational judgment on his special subject.

But there is a peril worse than this which we may encounter. The greatest writers of the world are enigmatic figures; they glimmer and loom in mists of controversy, and as

That Theban Monster that propos'd
Her riddle, and him, who solv'd it not, devour'd,

they propose problems to the world for which the world can find no answer. The question of Homer is enough to nonplus any student; but of the questionable shapes which may leap from our shelves and drag us off to their dens of dark obscurity, Dante and Shakespeare are more to be dreaded. But while Dante merely petrifies the brains of most Dante students, and turns them into pedants,[1] the attempt to solve the famous Shakespeare problem may deprive us altogether of our wits. And even if we escape this ultimate disaster, we shall find his figure, if we gaze too long upon it, grow to such proportions that other writers must be dwarfed and pushed aside.

The way, too, that Shakespeare has been made into a kind of national institution tends to make us hostile and suspicious: we feel inclined, as a recent critic has said, to tap the pedestal of this imposing statue; and gazing up at its vacuous face, we ask ourselves whether we are not, after all, being hoaxed. And when we do open a Shakespeare play, what rant we often find ourselves reading, what doggerel and dull jokes, what tedious writing! How the crude horseplay bores in the comedies, the hackneyed situations repeated over and over, the mirthless puns, and the intolerable chop-logic passing itself off as wit! What swollen rhetoric abounds in the historical plays, and how we are deafened by all the drum-and-trumpet business! The tragedies are full of melodrama, and holocausts of slaughter, and end, as Tolstoy said, with the dragging out by their legs of half-a-dozen corpses. How can we help feeling at times that 'repulsion, weariness and bewilderment,' which Tolstoy tells us he always felt when he read Shake-

---

[1] But Dante can be more dangerous sometimes; thus William Rossetti tells us how not only his father's mind, but his father's house in Charlotte Street was haunted by Dante as by a banshee, whose shriekings, however, had grown so familiar to the Rossetti children that they ceased to listen to them.

speare? The famous 'What? What?' of George III will sometimes echo in our ears. Was there ever in fact, as the Patriot King unpatriotically asked, 'such stuff as a great part of Shakespeare? Only,' he added, 'one must not say so.' But this crowned Shakespearean critic (who afterwards went mad) did say it. 'What! is there not sad stuff? What? What?' he barked at Fanny Burney.

Is there not indeed sad stuff? Must its writer be seriously regarded as the noblest of all poets, the glory of human nature, the greatest mind that has ever appeared among men, and the 'perfect boast of time'? This barbaric medley of bombast and ribaldry, of blood and melodrama—is this really the top of human achievement, the noblest memorial, as we are told, that our race can leave behind it of our existence on this planet? Can it be, as a great thinker has conjectured, that in their celestial colloquies the high authorities of the universe call the earth 'Shakespeare,' from the glory shed upon it by his genius which flashes afar through the interstellar spaces?

Can these things be? Or are we imposed upon, hocussed and bamboozled, the dupes of a gigantic Brocken-spectre of make-believe and mist, and victims, as Tolstoy so impressively maintained,[2] of a great collective

---

[2] Tolstoy's essay is published in *Tolstoy and Art* (Oxford Press). There can be no question of the complete sincerity of this very able anti-Shakespeare manifesto, in which Tolstoy describes the astonishment and consternation with which he, on reading Shakespeare's plays, had always found himself in complete disagreement with the received opinion of their merits. He had read them again and again,

hallucination, one of those crazes and epidemic manias, like the belief in witches or in the approaching end of the world, by which whole nations and whole ages have often been obsessed? Even the high priests of this established Shakespeare worship seem to betray, now and then, an uneasy consciousness of something equivocal about the object of their devotion; of things to be hushed up, and the need of whitewash.

II

The statue, indeed, looks all right—there he stands, 'our Shakespeare,' the great poet of Great Britain, and the volume he holds belongs, with the English Bible and the English Prayer Book, to the most sacred possessions of our race. In it we find the record of his genius, so myriad-minded and yet so English, with his joy in the English countryside and his appreciation of

---

he tells us; read them in English, read them in Russian and German translations; had discussed them over and over with Shakespeare enthusiasts, and at last, after a still more careful reperusal, he had found himself at the age of seventy-five faced with the alternative that either he or the world was mad, and had arrived at the 'final, indubitable, firm conviction,' that the world, with regard to Shakespeare, was the victim of one of those insane delusions, to which it always had been and always will be subject. Those deifications of Shakespeare he regarded (though he died before the War) as a piece of German propaganda, having been started by the German romantic writers for the purpose of liberating their drama from the tyranny of French ideals, thus substituting Shakespeare as a model which would leave them free to follow their own disorderly instincts and devices.

the bluff, honest qualities which make the inhabitants of this island what they are. He has, indeed, suffered much, has been through a time when the sorrows of the world have pressed heavily on his soul; but even in this dark period he never lost the fundamental sanity of his view of life; and his last years were spent in an atmosphere of reconciliation and quiet happiness, in the golden glow of an opulent and serene sunset of the spirit.

But the whitewash, alas, will keep flaking off and leave unsightly patches—the money-lending, for instance, and the petty lawsuits which occupied that evening of his years, and the second-best bed he bequeathed to his wife, as an afterthought, just when his sun was about to set. We can explain away this bed of his last bequest; we can also explain away his hurried marriage to its occupant in his youth; but what are we to do about those sonnets he was fond of writing, his brutal sonnets to the Dark Lady, and his sentimental sonnets to the Lovely Boy? The story Shakespeare recounts of his moral—or rather his immoral—predicament between these 'two loves' of his—

Two loves I have of comfort and despair—

must certainly, in the interests of the British Empire, be smothered up; the business of proving and reproving, and proving over again—and then proving still once more, just to be absolutely certain—that our Shakespeare cannot possibly mean what he so frankly tells us, has become almost a national industry.

And then, too, there is Shakespeare's ribaldry—the bawdy jokes he is so fond of making. Luckily, it is only the specialist who knows how much ribaldry there is in Shakespeare's plays, how many passages which seem innocent enough are full of double-meanings. 'He can't mean that!' the shocked reader exclaims; but oh, my dear reader, he does mean it, and his meaning, if you are a nice-minded person, will make you blush all over. The late Poet Laureate tried to palliate the offence on the ground that Shakespeare was compelled against his will to season in this gross way the plays he wrote for his gross audience; but Robert Bridges did not explain the recondite improprieties which must have been far above the vulgar apprehension, and the indelicacies with which he spiced the sugared sonnets written for his private friends. A gross age, no doubt, but Sidney and Spenser wrote no sonnets of this kind. Even worse than this ithyphallic fun in which Shakespeare so plainly delighted, is the evidence of a more distressing kind of sex-preoccupation, by which, during a certain period of his life, he seems to have been obsessed. Lear's obscene railings against the mere fact of sex, which are quite inappropriate to his circumstances and situation, and in which he seems to scream and spit from horror, and Timon's even more terrible outbursts of sex-nausea, sound like the incoherent ravings of an unbalanced mind, driven to madness by a loathing for men and women in their natural intercourse together.

Difficult also to explain away is the moral callousness

which Shakespeare often shows, not only in the physical atrocities he sometimes exhibits on the stage—the 'Out, vile jelly!' for instance, of Gloster's blinding—but in the moral outrages he perpetrates upon our feelings— the way he pardons, or rather ignores, unpardonable things; mates his heroines to dastards, and brings more than one of his plays by an ugly bed-trick to an ugly conclusion.[3]

It is impossible to get rid of the suspicion that of all

[3] A list of the atrocities, the offences against taste, morals, and any kind of decent feeling, which are to be found in the canon of the Folio, and which are accepted as Shakespeare's work by his adorers, is enough to prove—if more proof were needed—what enormities the orthodox can swallow, apparently without a gulp, in their Sacred Writings. Otherwise the belief that Shakespeare wrote that disgusting record of more than beastly horror, *Titus Andronicus*, within a year or so of writing *A Midsummer Night's Dream*, would burst their brains; nor would they find it easy to digest Shakespeare's treatment of Joan of Arc in the scene (1 *Henry VI*, V, iv) where the Maid of France, to escape burning, declares herself to be with child, first by one, and then by another of the French Princes. The wager of Posthumus about the chastity of Imogen, the slaughter of the unarmed Hector at the instigation of Achilles in *Troilus and Cressida*, and indeed the ugly degradation of all the Greek heroes in that magnificent but unpleasant play, would turn the stomachs of less devout readers. The marriage of Celia to that scoundrel Oliver, in *As You Like It*, and that of Hero to the despicable Claudio in *Much Ado*, are bad enough, but as an outrage on our moral feelings few things in literature can equal the scene in the *Two Gentlemen of Verona*, where Valentine makes an outrageous and calm offer of Silvia, whom he loves, to the scoundrel whose attempt to outrage her he has just prevented. Shakespeare was apt to end off his plays, it is true, by any unscrupulous contrivance, but this plea can hardly be urged to palliate the cold-blooded rejection of Falstaff; and the only excuse which can be found for the degradation of that master-spirit into the poor dupe and buffoon of the *Merry Wives*, is to label as 'sentimentalists' those who do not like it.

great artists Shakespeare was the most completely devoid of all artistic conscience; that he was perfectly willing to make any sacrifice for the sake of stage-effect, money, and popular applause. One cannot but think of him and the other Elizabethan dramatists as being not unlike pastry-cooks who concoct their pies with little thought of anything but their sale to the customer of the day, and who are not in the least scrupulous about the ingredients they put into them.

III

The fact is well known that writing for the stage was not regarded as literature in Shakespeare's time. The drama existed to supply that popular demand for mental recreation which sates itself today with newspapers, magazines, murder stories and the cinema; and new plays, hot and hot, were constantly needed. A play, however successful, never had a 'run,' and was repeated at the most seven or eight times a year. They were regarded for the most part as being of but ephemeral interest; and though, like sermons, one might be occasionally printed, the greater part of them have probably perished; the less than seven hundred Elizabethan plays which survive probably representing but a small proportion of those which were written, and even of those which were produced. Their writers, who had to furnish them as fast as they were needed, much as a modern journalist has to furnish a certain amount of copy at a certain date, worked in haste, and had small time for revision; and once paid for their work, did not as a rule trouble themselves about the fate of their compositions. Not literary reputation, but the crowded theatre was their reward.

What an amazing phenomenon by the way is the Elizabethan drama! The sudden outburst of passionate, imaginative rhetoric and unbounded poetic imagination, which flared up for so brief a period, and in twenty years passed, as it has been said, 'from the fiery dawn of Marlowe to the silvered dusk of Massinger'—what literary phenomenon in our own, or in any literary history is comparable in its strangeness and splendour to this? Sir Walter Raleigh gives a most vivid picture of it in his *Shakespeare;* how the beginnings of popular drama already existed in the London of the eighties, with its clowns and jugglers and players and authors of dramatic interludes, who had grown prosperous by their popular success; and how this flaunting underworld was invaded by a band of reckless young men from the universities, not scholars in any strict sense, but 'who had been caught by the Latin poets, and were eager students of the new literature of the Renaissance in Italy, France, and Spain.' They came to live by their wits in London, first of all as hack-writers for the booksellers; but they soon became acquainted with the flaunting vagabonds of the stage, the 'harlotry players,' as Mrs. Quickly called them, who were both actors and dramatic writers, and

who, finding their old interludes and Morality Plays
falling out of fashion, felt there was room for the new
inventions of these scholars; took them to live among
them, and made them acquainted with the 'lewdest persons of the land.'

Of these university men Marlowe was the king;
'already, before his arrival, Lyly had shown the way to
make classical mythology engaging, and Peele had used
blank verse so that it rang in the ear and dwelt in the
memory.' But 'the work of these men was designed for
select courtly circles, and left the wider public un-
touched. Marlowe appealed to the people. He brought
blank verse on to the public stage and sent it echoing
through the town.' Marlowe not only made classical
fable popular, but he imagined great and serious actions
and splendid passions and heroic characters. The success of his *Tamburlaine* in 1587 is perhaps, Sir Walter
Raleigh says, the greatest event in our literary history.
His friends and fellows, Peele and Greene and Nashe,
recognized his triumph, and followed his lead to claim
a share in his success. Out they poured it all, stately
masques, and Italianate, Arcadian Pastorals, comedy,
coarseness, ribaldry and splendid declamation, and above
all that world of terror and horror, which in the ancient
and Renaissance theatre was by prescription allotted to
tragedy. 'The mandates and kings,' as the phrase of
Scaliger has it, 'slaughters, despairs, executions, exiles,
loss of parents, parricides, incests, conflagrations, battles,

loss of sight, tears, shrieks, lamentations, burials, epitaphs and funeral songs.' [4]

What a seething cauldron of blood, ghosts, horror, grossness and splendid poetry it all is!

If we want to catch the thrill of witnessing such a drama in the 'wooden O,' as Shakespeare calls it, the 'round,' the 'ring,' 'Cock-pit,' of a little old theatre, long ago, one winter day in London, we shall find it most vividly described in Marston's famous Prologue to *Antonio's Revenge*, when, after describing the dank of 'clumsy' winter, with its sleet and snarling gusts, he adds,

> *O now, methinks, a sullen tragic scene*
> *Would suit the time with pleasing congruence . . .*
> *Therefore, we proclaim,*
> *If any spirit breathes within this round,*
> *Uncapable of weighty passion, . . .*
> *Who winks, and shuts his apprehension up*
> *From common sense of what men were and are,*
> *Who would not know what men must be—let such*
> *Hurry amain from our black-visaged shows:*
> *We shall affright their eyes. But if a breast*
> *Nail'd to the earth with grief; if any heart*
> *Pierc'd through with anguish pant within this ring;*
> *If there be any blood whose heat is choked*
> *And stifled with true sense of misery;*
> *If ought of these strains fill this consort up—*
> *Th' arrive most welcome.*

[4] I don't pretend that I have read Scaliger, or that I ever shall. I have borrowed this quotation from Professor Stoll's *Hamlet*, p. 65 n.

But what now remains of all this sudden brief blaze of poetry, rhetoric and passion? Lamb and our romantic critics revelled in it, but the world has found it for the most part too wild, chaotic, noisy and incoherent, too lacking in restraint and intellectual substance, to win for itself, in spite of Marlowe, Webster, Ford, Dekker, Heywood and the others, an assured place with the Greek, the French, and even with the Spanish drama, in the literature of the world. It blazed up and it died down; the intellectuals of the time paid no serious attention to it, and today only a few readers and scholars rake over, now and then, its still-fiery ashes. For us its real interest is the splendid accident of Shakespeare's appearance, which glorified the Elizabethan drama, and yet in a way robbed it of its glory; the way he shone out and eclipsed those fellow playwrights of his; 'how far,' in Lamb's phrase, 'in his divine mind and manners he surpassed them and all mankind.' But one thing may be said, that to understand Shakespeare's greatness, and to what heights he soars above his contemporaries, it pays, or almost pays, a person of infinite astronomical leisure like myself to read, as I have read, the Elizabethan drama as a preliminary to reading Shakespeare; to explore first the foothills from among which that great summit rises.

IV

Ben Jonson was the only dramatic writer of that time who, with the exception perhaps of Lyly, was blessed,

or (as it has been suggested) cursed with an artistic conscience, and who had any feeling for the dignity of his
profession, or solicitude about the future of his plays.
His fellows ridiculed him for the time and toil he gave
to his compositions; and when he published them in
1616, he confounded both his friends and enemies by
the audacity of calling them his *Works* on the title page.
Works! So grave, so stately, so dignified a title, reserved
for great classical writers, great scholars, and grave
theologians, printed on the title-page of a collection of
mere stage-plays! The indignation and laughter lasted
for many years, and the editors of Shakespeare did not
dare to use the word on the title-page of the Folio, and
only insinuated it on a later page, where it was not likely
to attract any general attention.

These editors praise Shakespeare for his haste in
composition; he had never blotted a line, they declared
proudly ('Would he had blotted a thousand!' Ben
Jonson retorts). In fact, although Shakespeare took his
long poems seriously, and saw to their careful printing,
he does not seem to have regarded his plays as serious
performances, and to have taken any pride in acknowl-
edging them—indeed, the first editions of his separate
plays were published anonymously, and to the printing
of none of the quartos which came out in his life-time
did he give the least attention.[5]

[5] For the above account of the drama in Shakespeare's time, I am
indebted to Professor Lounsbury's brilliant and fascinating book,
The Text of Shakespeare (Scribner, 1906). Published in England
under a different title, *The First Editors of Shakespeare.*

V

It is no considerations of the kind of which I have been writing, however, which make me hesitate before reading Shakespeare. His hasty composition and hasty marriage do not disconcert me, nor the money-lending nor the bedstead; I don't mind the ribaldry, I rather like it,[6] and in the Sonnets I find described a sex-quandary which psycho-analysis has taught us to regard as not at all unusual. Although, as a matter of personal taste, I love best those artists who, like Virgil or Milton, love and respect their art, and seek to attain perfection in it, I am not too narrow-minded to enjoy the careless prodigality of the great purveyors who employ their divine gifts in catering for the public. Great art is great

[6] That is, when I can understand it, which is by no means always easy. Thus the orchard scene in *Romeo and Juliet*, when Juliet rebukes Romeo for swearing by 'the moon, the inconstant moon'— this most exquisite of scenes is prefaced by a speech of Mercutio's full of double-meanings which the most earnest and impure-minded thinkers find it difficult to understand. Even when I was able at last to sit under the medlar tree and join in the learned giggles about

> *That kind of fruit*
> *As maids call medlars, when they laugh alone,*

I was for a long time baffled by the two lines which follow—lines held to be so atrocious that they are the only ones omitted in several otherwise unexpurgated editions of Shakespeare's plays. The best course for those seriously interested in this branch of Shakespearean research, is to study the notes of some frank eighteenth-century edition, or collate our modern text with the Bowdlerized text of the wily old Bowdler, and notice the passages he omits or changes. The keenness of Bowdler's wicked old nose has deservedly won for his name a place in our English vocabulary.

art, in whatever workshop it is fashioned and for however mercenary a purpose. Molière and Scott and
Dickens wrote for the market, and many of the immortal painters of the Renaissance actually kept shops,
in which they turned out their masterpieces in the ordinary way of business.

What, however, does make me uneasy is a certain
misgiving—not about Shakespeare, but about myself.
Granted that his work deserves all the praise which has
been lavished on it, are we in the fitting mood just now
to appreciate that splendour? We are all the children
of our age: we cannot help it; and in the East wind
which prevails today have we the high spirits to enjoy
Shakespeare's boisterous fun? Shall we not find our ears
out of tune for his sweet music; and may not his pretty
boy-and-girl romances seem rather insipid to our taste?
And, above all, will his pathos still move us; and if it
does move us, may it not be in a way that we resent?

Pathos, the power of touching our tender feelings,
has always been one of the great gifts of the greatest
writers; there is noble pathos in Homer, in Virgil, and
in Dante, and again and again in the voices of the most
famous novelists the sound of a sob is heard.[7] None of

[7] How highly this gift of pathos was esteemed by the Victorian
novelists is illustrated by an anecdote which Leslie Stephen recounts
with no ironic intention. When George Eliot, he tells us, had shown
in her first story that she could write good dialogue, it was still a
question whether she had the command of pathos. The doubt was
settled, however, by her description of the last illness of Mrs. Barton.
She and Lewes both wept over this scene, and Lewes kissed her,
exclaiming: 'I think your pathos is better than your fun.'

our modern writers dare, however, to touch that string: we are lacking in the sensibility which responds with gratitude to such appeals. Now Shakespeare is certainly the most moving of all writers, the greatest master of pathos the world has ever known. No one can unlock the source of tears and wring the heart as he wrings it; and I must confess that I find the harrowing scenes in Shakespeare, like the scene between Arthur and Hubert in *King John,* or the slaughter of Macduff's children, or the deaths of Lear and Desdemona, intolerable—I cannot bear them; and even scenes which are not quite so harrowing: Desdemona's Willow Song, for instance, or Ophelia's madness, I find 'shy-making,' to use a new-invented phrase.

Perhaps the Elizabethans were made of sterner stuff than we are, and did not mind being hit below the belt; or perhaps they wore their belts lower than we wear them. Or it may be that our inability to enjoy such appeals to the emotions is due to some temporary exasperation of the spirit from which the spirit will recover? Or, I sometimes wonder, may it not be the inevitable effect of modern science on our modern world-outlook? If remorse and agony and vehement passion are regarded no longer as moral, but as pathological phenomena, how can those who so regard them be moved by the pity and terror on which, as Aristotle said, tragedy is based? With the loss of our belief in the responsibility of the free agent, have we lost also the tragic sense of life? We may feel that life is meaningless and hateful, we may be exasperated to desperation by it; but when from our desolate vision of the cosmos we turn to the glowing and highly-coloured world of Shakespeare's, the poet of Free Will, full as it is of moral tragedies and triumphs, of vehement will and ardour and agony, may it not seem a tempest in an inconsiderable cup which it is superfluous for us to augment with our tears?

VI

All these fine reasons which I allege to myself for not reading Shakespeare are, however, I know quite well, little more than rationalizations, as they are called, of indolence; high-sounding excuses in which my dread of the difficulty of the task seeks to hide its head. For plays, unlike novels, demand close attention, they demand a certain effort of the mind and the imagination; and Shakespeare's plays, above all, require study: his vocabulary is full of obsolete words and idioms; and his writing, especially in the later plays, is sometimes so involved and obscure, so rapid and abrupt, that we cannot understand it. To read and only half-comprehend what one is reading hardly seems a satisfactory method of perusal; while to pause and consult a glossary and pore over one note after another fatigues and distracts the attention. And even these notes of the annotators will often add to our embarrassment. Every line and every word in the text of Shakespeare has been exposed

to the fiercest light of criticism; and his commentators
have discovered, for the confusion of the perplexed
reader, almost innumerable difficulties which he would
never have noticed for himself.

> *Thy tooth is not so keen,*
> *Because thou art not seen—*

when Amiens addresses the winter wind in these words,
or when Feste sings:

> *Then come kiss me, sweet and twenty,*

or the Duke, in *Twelfth Night,* says of music:

> *Give me excess of it, that, surfeiting,*
> *The appetite may sicken, and so die,*

the common reader is perplexed to learn that these simple lines present problems difficult to solve, and that
when Lear threatens to make a 'sop o' the moonshine'
of Goneril's steward, when Hamlet calls the King 'a
pajock,' or Theseus speaks of his 'sanded' hounds, or
Lorenzo of the 'patines of bright gold' which inlay the
floor of heaven, no one knows for certain what they
mean.

And we are told, also, that when we think we are
reading Shakespeare we may not be reading him at all.
His authorship of several of the plays assigned to him
is doubtful; and even of those which are esteemed the
most authentic we possess no authentic text, and cannot
be sure of the accuracy of a single line. They have come

down to us in a state of manifest and admitted corruption: all we possess is a set of prompt-books used by a particular troupe of actors for a particular audience. And, worse than all this, the view has come to be widely held that Shakespeare seldom wrote original plays: that it was his business rather to re-cast and furbish up old plays already in the repertory of his theatre; and that in the text of these, as we possess them, there remains not only much of the writing of their first authors, but layer after layer of subsequent additions. How far this process of disintegration of Shakespeare's text is a valid one, and to what results it may lead us, no one at present can possibly say. The battle between the disintegrators and the defenders of the accepted text, 'foliolators, growing desperate in their doomed undertaking'—so they are described by their opponents—is raging just now more fiercely than ever.

Even more formidable are the barriers which another set of critics have erected between Shakespeare and his readers. Shakespeare's plays, they tell us, were not written to be read, but acted, and to read them is to miss their true significance and meaning. They are performances, designed for the eyes and ears of their spectators, moving pageants of action, sound, and colour; the texts we possess are like operatic scores: to read one of these is at the best but reading the score of an opera and trying to hum its tunes. And even if we do succeed in re-creating in imagination the play as a stage performance, our difficulties are by no means over.

The stage of Shakespeare's time was so totally different from the stage as we know it, that we distort and disfigure his plays if we place them upon our stage, whether in imagination or actual performance. To understand Shakespeare, therefore, we must fit ourselves out with Elizabethan eyes and ears; must stand beneath the open sky in an enclosure hardly larger than a tennis-court, 'to see a boy-Lady Macbeth act before a curtain declaring itself to be a royal palace.' We must in fact reconstruct for ourselves the Elizabethan stage, and master the art of stagecraft as it was practised in Shakespeare's time. But as this is at present impossible, and, indeed, may always be so, since our knowledge of the Elizabethan stage is, and is likely to remain, very incomplete, any attempt to re-create the tunes of Shakespeare's scores is like an attempt to recover the music of ancient instruments without knowing what sounds they actually did emit.

But this is by no means the worst of our predicament. As the approach to the great temples of Egypt is guarded by avenues of lions with human faces, who are supposed to tear their enemies to pieces, so the approach to the temple of Shakespeare-worship is beset by sphinxes who are quite as ready to dismember and devour those who give wrong answers to their questions. Of all the sphinxes of the East, the biggest of course is that great monster, 190 feet long, of Gizeh, which gazes across the Valley of the Nile, and guards the entrance to it; almost as formidable to me is a modern monster of the Middle West which has recently heaved up her bulk in America, and stands with her avenue of daughter-sphinxes, gazing across the Mississippi Valley. For, according to this new-born school of critics, we must, if we wish to understand Shakespeare and the problems he presents, not only fit our heads with Elizabethan eyes and ears, but must furnish them inside with Elizabethan brains as well. The modern idea of Shakespeare, according to these critics, is nothing but a windy, vast balloon, inflated by German and Scotch professors, by literary gents of leisure, minor poets and writers of closet-plays ('let rude ears,' as Milton somewhere says, 'be absent'), by propagandists, idealists and blatherskites, who have combined to distend and blow it up with the hot air of modern transcendentalism, sentimentality, psychology and introspection—all things of which, of course, the Elizabethans had not the slightest notion. Shakespeare was one of these Elizabethans; he was not 'a prophet, living in the spirit of the nineteenth century while working in the sixteenth'; not a thinker voyaging through strange seas of thought alone, but a jolly old actor and playwright, who filled his borrowed plots with fine acting parts and thrilling situations, all concocted to suit the taste and temper of the time. To understand them we must understand that taste and temper, and realise that the meaning of these plays—their only meaning—is their surface meaning, as Shakespeare's contemporaries understood it. Shakespeare in writing his plays had in fact, they say, no subtle intentions and no deep underlying ideas; his characters were little more than the stock figures of the renascence stage. Falstaff is, and was meant to be, a coward, a liar and boaster, 'a false, fat, tavern rogue, dissolute, scurillous and worthless'; Shylock is the hated Jew, and butt of the time, meant to be mocked at, spat upon, and dismissed at last with vindictive laughter and contempt. That Othello falls a prey at once to Iago's calumnies is not in the least due to any tragic flaw in his character, but simply to the universally accepted stage-convention that the calumniator is always believed at once, however incredible his calumnies may be. This can be proved, they say, by instances out of the whole history of the drama, from the age of Greece down to the nineteenth century; and indeed, according to this school, the great sin of criticism is to judge works of art, not by other works of art, but by life, with which they have little or no connection. In fact all the profound or mystical meanings we read into Shakespeare's plays are absurd anachronisms, about as irrelevant and absurd as the mystical relations between Christ and his spouse, the Church, which theologians read into those outspoken old erotic lyrics collected in the *Song of Songs*.

The leader of this American and hardest-boiled of all the hard-boiled schools of Shakespeare criticism, is a learned and out-spoken American professor, Professor Elmer Edgar Stoll, Ph.D., of Minneapolis.[8] Professor

[8] Professor Stoll has published one volume on Shakespeare, *Shakespeare Studies* (The Macmillan Company, N. Y., 1927), and several

Stoll is one of the most erudite of living Shakespeare scholars, and possesses also an accurate and unrivalled knowledge of dramatic history—of the Greek, the Latin, the Spanish, the Italian, the French and English theatres, and his scholarship is accompanied, as all sound scholarship should be accompanied, by a vigorous gift of vituperation; it is he, for instance, who has added to the vocabulary of Shakespearean criticism the word 'blatherskite'—'a talker of blatant nonsense,' as the dictionary defines it. I have incorporated above into my genteel prose, one or two of his less striking phrases. Altogether an awkward customer, a fierce eagle in the fluttered dovecotes, a wolf in the quiet fold of literary professors, and one who is moved to derision and no pity by their cooings and transcendental bleatings. And yet, as the erudite historian of Shakespeare criticism admits with the sigh of one who prefers the old romantic method—Professor Stoll, whom he describes as among the first of contemporary critics, is, with his businesslike methods, 'pointing the highway to the best criticism of the future.' [9]

papers of importance, *Anachronism in Shakespeare Criticism* (Modern Philology, 1918), *Othello*, in the *Studies of Language and Literature* of the University of Minnesota, 1915, and *Hamlet*, in the same (1919), and *The Tempest*, in the Publications of the Modern Language Association of America (September, 1932). His latest volume, *Poets and Playwrights* (University of Minnesota Press), contains several essays on Shakespeare of great interest.

[9] *Shakespearian Criticism*, Augustus Ralli, Oxford Press, Vol. II, p. 258.

VII

Many are the problems, as we have seen, both of text
and interpretation, that meet the would-be reader of
Shakespeare's plays. Of these problems, these Theban
monsters threatening to devour those who cannot solve
their riddles, two there are which have always perplexed me most, for the great Sonnet Problem I refuse
to face. 'There are so many footprints,' as Sir Walter
Raleigh grimly remarks, 'around the cave of this mystery, none of them pointing in the outward direction.'
The first of these is what is called the Dark Period
Problem, and the relation in general between Shakespeare's life and his plays; and the second is the problem of stage-representation—whether we best appreciate
these plays by reading them, or by watching their performance on the stage. I hope, before I finish this essay,
to try to face these two monsters, but in the meantime,
Professor Stoll has raised a still more (to me at least)
perplexing problem. Is it true, he makes us ask ourselves, that to understand and appreciate Shakespeare
we must pop him back into his own age, judge his plays
by the plays of his contemporaries and see life through
the eyes with which he and they saw it? Is it not the
business of the critic to help the reader to become the
contemporary of the writer whose works he is reading,
rather than to alchemize and etherealize and sentimen-
talize those works into contemporary writings? Can they

possess beauties of which their author had no notion, and above all ideas that were perfectly unknown both to himself and to the age he lived in? Should we not then search for the truth, rather than invent and seek to impart it, and study Shakespeare, not by the light of modern, personal, temperamental impressions, which may mean anything, everything—which may mean nothing at all—but, sacrificing on the altar of sacred truth, all this 'sentimental finery,' as our Professor calls it, read Shakespeare's plays only and austerely by the light, so dim to us, by which, after long research, we have come to believe he wrote them?

How shall I face this and the other Theban monsters, how answer their dark riddles and not be eaten up?

I have found it. Oh, happy answer! Why read Shakespeare at all? No one else reads him; why should I alone be forced to undertake the task? There is nothing about it in the Ten Commandments; no Voice from Mount Sinai has put this obligation on me; and if such a voice should shout it in my ears, could I not justifiably reply that the thing is impossible in the present state of things?

That just simply it can't be done?

And as for writing about Shakespeare, heaven preserve me from so mad and desperate an undertaking! Am I to climb all the insuperable fences, push my way through the impenetrable thickets, defy these formidable sphinxes, only to have 'blatherskite' shouted at me from the Middle West?

Let me alone, let me enjoy in peace my comforts and declining years. And anyhow, what with the brevity of those years, and with bridge, and going out to lunch, and all the modern murder-stories to occupy my so-called mind at home, how in heaven's name can I ever find time to read Shakespeare?

VIII

In one of his letters Henry James describes how ignobly fond he had become as he grew older of not travelling; 'to keep up not doing it,' he writes, 'is in itself for me the most thrilling of adventures.' So not to read Shakespeare, not to travel into his kingdom, but to sneak up at night towards the barriers that guard its frontier, and lurk there, terrified by the thought of the dangers I might encounter if I did really enter in, has become for me also a thrilling if not very noble adventure.

It may sound absurd to speak of danger in connection with a region which, in spite of a few geographical uncertainties, is so written up in hand-books, so betrod by tourists, so well provided with beaten roads and signposts and official guides. But it is a region, nevertheless, full of dark pitfalls for the mind; tangled thickets there are of significant, as well as textual interpretation; mazes of thought in which many wander and find no issue, and many paths whitened by the bleaching bones of critics. On one side of the beaten track, with its char-àbancs full of tourists, its files of boys and girls from the secondary schools, personally conducted by their teachers, lies the abyss I have mentioned of the great Dark Period; on the other, the Serbonian sonnet-bog, in which armies whole have sunk; while the attempt to reconcile the poetry which Shakespeare wrote with the prose of the extremely prosaic life he led is apt to addle the brains of those who undertake it. Shaken and appalled by the thought of this Apollo as an actor and jovial stage-manager in a little old London theatre—a mere bare room with a blanket for a curtain—this demigod serenely running a popular show and raking in the pennies—this thought stupefies them, and they are seized with a kind of vertigo. Of the inhabitants of the insane asylums of Great Britain it has been calculated that, after the religious maniacs, the two next largest classes consist of those who rave about the Royal Family, or those who, by thinking about Shakespeare, have unhinged their minds.

A great divine of the Elizabethan age describes in one of his sermons a region in the East, in Georgia, which was so immersed all day in gloom that no one could see his own hand within its borders; those who dwelt upon its frontiers could hear, he said, the noise of cocks crowing, horses neighing, and the cries of human beings, but no one outside dared to venture in for fear of losing his way in that land of eternal darkness. Thus the cries of the distracted inhabitants sometimes reach us from the dark realm of Shakespeare interpretation. We hear the bleating of idiot adorers and the eternal swish of their whitewash brushes; we hear the squeals of the idealists and blatherskites as Professor Stoll pigsticks them; the war-cries of the Foliolaters and Disintegrators as they rush upon each other; and even wilder battle cries than these (for it is impossible to exaggerate their strangeness) will reach our ears. For listen! the fanatic followers of no less than five ghostly, resurrected Elizabethan Earls are shouting at each other, the two bands of Pembrokians and Southamptonites, each vociferating that their Lord was the inspirer of the Sonnets, while three other bands proclaim the more glorious boast (at least more glorious to some thinkers) that Lord Derby, or Lord Rutland, or Lord Oxford, was the author of them, and of Shakespeare's plays as well. And then, faint and far, as the wind shifts, we hear the ululations of those vaster herds of Baconian believers, as they plunge squeaking down the Gadarene slope of their delusion.[10]

Yes, on the whole I feel that I am against Shakespeare—the vast subject is too vexatious, too intricate and baffling. Though I may not join with Tolstoy and

---

[10] I do not wish, however, to speak with any disrespect of that view of the authorship of Shakespeare's plays which is so firmly held by officers in the Navy and the Army, by one of His Majesty's judges, and the manager of more than one large drapery establishment, and is corroborated by the authority of Mark Twain, Mrs. Henry Pott, Prince Bismarck, John Bright, the late Mr. Crump, K.C., and several thoughtful baronets.

Bernard Shaw, and shout 'Down with Shakespeare!' in the streets, I shall nevertheless keep well aloof from the grounds of that great lunatic asylum, that dark domain of ghosts and pedants, of blatherskites, monomaniacs, fanatics and fools.

THE GREAT ADVENTURE

Chapter II

THE GREAT ADVENTURE

BUT THEN, from over the borders of the region I have been describing, there float the echoes of an aerial music: 'Come unto these yellow sands': 'O mistress mine, where are you roaming?' 'What is love? 'Tis not hereafter,' 'Fear no more the heat o' the sun'—those words thrill in my ears, and often the mere gleam of a Shakespearean phrase lights up with a sudden illumination the alien page on which I find it.

Critics have often noticed the extraordinary effect of Shakespeare in quotation; how his words possess beyond all other words a potency, and exert a spell which thrills our imagination.

> Let determin'd things to destiny
> Hold unbewail'd their way—

> O! now, for ever
> Farewell the tranquil mind; farewell content!
> Farewell the plumèd troop and the big wars—

> In the most high and palmy state of Rome,
> A little ere the mightiest Julius fell,

> O Proserpina!
> For the flowers now that frighted thou let'st fall
> From Dis's waggon! daffodils,

That come before the swallow dares, and take
The winds of March with beauty; violets dim—

How silver-sweet sound lovers' tongues by night—

Now what am I to do about it? The mere first lines
of certain plays—

If music be the food of love, play on—

When shall we three meet again—

In sooth, I know not why I am so sad—

Such lines open for me portals into realms of beauty
and fear and strangeness; and as I recall the impressions of my former visits, a kind of longing, a home-
sickness for that world of the imagination grows upon
me. What, on a mind grown older, will be the effect,
I ask myself, of an experience which in earlier years
had been so passionate, so intense? Shall I find disillu-
sion there, or a richer and more profound appreciation?
Youth is the time for the adventures of the body, but
age for the triumphs of the mind; and no triumph of
the mind can be greater than that of reaching in
thought a peak of speculation, and of obtaining thence
a view, clear and luminous and comprehensive, of some
half-explored region; of grasping something so vast
and complex as that which the phenomenon we call
Shakespeare presents.

I find it an interest in life—perhaps the greatest of
my interests—and one which, as I grow older, grows

both in intensity, and in my power to satisfy it—to provide my mind with meanings to attach to names. I travel to make for myself clear pictures for the names of famous and foreign cities, I study to form clear conceptions in which, as in cabinets of shining glass, I can treasure up and keep in mind the wonders of thought and letters. To form adequate conceptions of all things which come within the scope of our intelligence—has not one of the greatest of philosophers told us that this is the ultimate aim of life, in the satisfaction of which the happiness and blessedness of man alone consists? 'A man who has not read Homer,' Bagehot said, 'is like a man who has not seen the ocean. There is a great object of which he has no idea.' I want to have an idea of Shakespeare; to understand what the word 'Shakespearean' means. Though I shan't be able, of course, to solve the Shakespeare problems, I may learn at least what these problems are; and at any rate I shall discover what Shakespeare means to me; what, when sitting alone, with my ears shut to the reverberations of his fame, I really think and feel about him. My cup may not be a big one, but it is my own; what, I wonder, shall I find there when I have once more dipped it into that rushing stream of sound? 'How dull it is,' as the old Ulysses says in Tennyson's poem, 'to pause, to make an end!' The ocean of Shakespeare lies before me; 'there gloom the dark broad seas.' I grow eager to attempt this voyage of great adventure, to explore this great kingdom of the mind; and with the wise consideration of an experienced voyager I begin to overhaul my gear and pack my bag.

II

Whether there are sailors who sail without charts is doubtful, but there certainly are travellers who prefer to journey with no map to guide them, and readers who are contemptuous of books about books. They gain no profit, they say, by looking at things through the eyes of others. But this impromptu, uninstructed way of grasping at masterpieces in spontaneous leaps of feeling is but a poor way of learning how to enjoy them. The first surprise and flush of prompt delight is, of course, of great, perhaps the greatest, value; but a true appreciation is based on something more than feeling: it demands that we should not only enjoy, but understand our pleasure, and make it food for thought; should learn the esthetic reasons for it, and learn also all we can about the origins and environments of the monuments and masterpieces we gaze on. To understand them we must know their place in history, and their relative position among other masterpieces. And I at least find that my vision of the things I like is greatly enhanced and clarified by seeing them reflected in the luminous minds of other people. Esthetic appreciation is, luckily, a thing that can be communicated, can be learnt from others—the glow of it is a catching fire. How often an admiration spoken of by someone we ad-

mire—sometimes the mere mention of a preference—
has opened for us the gate into a new world of beauty!
And certainly the debt I owe to the great interpreters
of literature is far too large to allow me to join in the
common abuse of critics; they have given me ears, they
have given me eyes, they have taught me—and have
taught all of us really—the best way of appreciating
excellence, and how and where to find it. How many
sights unguided travellers pass by! how many beauties
readers of great works will miss, if they refuse to read
the books about them!

Thousands and thousands of books have been written
about Shakespeare, and most of them are mad. These
books are all very much alike in form and method.
Their introductions and first chapters are often good.
Each author begins by a sane and sensible exposure of
some folly of a predecessor; and then, little by little,
in hints and intimations, he begins to develop a delusion
of his own. Strange interpretations, sometimes crypto-
grams, appear at first in furtive footnotes, and then
flourish in the text; until at last the writer proclaims to
the world his great discovery with shouts of maniacal
exultation.

Luckily, however, all those who have written about
Shakespeare have not lost their reason: there is a select
library of wise and sane and scholarly books on the
subject. I know of few things more delightful than a
choice library, or rather a well-filled bookcase, of wise
books of Shakespeare criticism. What good reading they

are! Shakespeare has often been described as being like Nature herself; and certainly he seems like Nature, a subject that no study can exhaust. Each new effort of sound investigation so surely reveals a new aspect of his work, and so often sheds a fresh light on some familiar character or situation, that we feel—and feel with delight—that the interpretation of Shakespeare is indeed an endless adventure; that there remains an almost infinite number of new aspects for future critics to reveal.[1]

Of these wise books about Shakespeare, which I pack up to take with me for my expedition, the first that I choose, and all wise travellers should choose, is Dr. A. C. Bradley's *Shakespearean Tragedy* (Macmillan) —a book which, in spite of a certain amount of oversubtle interpretation now somewhat out of date, remains one of the greatest masterpieces of English criticism. I take, too, the beautiful and wayward volume of Swinburne (the 'most inspired,' as he has been described, 'and the most errant of critics'), *A Study of Shakespeare* (Scribner); and Coleridge, of course, travels with me. He is often an almost intolerable bore as a companion, but the 'flashes of his dark lantern' are sometimes more illuminating than those of any other

---

[1] 'Caliban has not yet been thoroughly fathomed. For all Shakespeare's great creations are like works of nature, subjects of unexhaustible study' (De Quincey's essay on Shakespeare).

For the latest and perhaps the best study of this strange and fascinating creature, see Professor Stoll's paper on *The Tempest*, mentioned above (p. 26).

light. I pack up Sir Edmund Chambers' *Shakespeare: A Survey* (Oxford Press) and the two volumes of Mr. Granville-Barker's *Prefaces to Shakespeare* (Sidgwick & Jackson), and only wish that more of these invaluable essays were printed; I take also Barrett Wendell's *William Shakespeare* (Scribner), and two small volumes which have been published recently, John Bailey's *Shakespeare* (Longmans), and Mr. Mackail's *Approach to Shakespeare* (Oxford Press). For biographies, I have with me Walter Raleigh's brief *Life* in the English Men of Letters Series, and the longer one of Joseph Quincey Adams, *A Life of William Shakespeare* (Houghton Mifflin), which saves me the burden of Sidney Lee's portentous biography. Of books by foreigners I pack up Schüking's *Character Problems in Shakespeare's Plays* (Holt), and the great volume of George Brandes, *William Shakespeare* (Macmillan), which Professor Herford has described as being, of all recent books on Shakespeare, 'the richest in wit and temperament, in luminous aperçus and dangerous assumptions, in felicitous suggestion and fascinating error.' Of the other books which I have found useful I give the list in an Appendix.

III

What exactly is the debt which we owe to the critics of Shakespeare, to the great succession of scholars and investigators who in the last one hundred and fifty years have so minutely studied his works? It is a debt surely beyond almost all computation. In the first place, there has been that settlement of the text of the plays which has been accomplished by successive generations of critics and scholars. Shakespeare, it has been truly said, is the only great author since the invention of printing who stands in the same position as those who flourished in the age of manuscripts. The quartos of his plays which were published in his life-time were printed without his supervision; the Folio of 1623 was most carelessly edited; it swarmed with misprints and unintelligible passages; the three Folios which followed were mere booksellers' reprints, with a few corrections it is true, but with more errors added; the text had seriously deteriorated in the hundred years after Shakespeare's death; even Rowe's edition of 1709, though it made some improvements, was not much better than the fourth Folio of 1685 on which it was founded, while Pope, in his disgraceful edition of 1725, mutilated the text, or made additions to it in the most amazing manner. Theobald was the first scholarly editor of Shakespeare in the modern sense, the first to make any real collation of the sources of the text, or any examination of contemporary Elizabethan literature to explain its meaning. He was also an emendator of real genius, and has added to the accepted text more happy readings—some of great brilliance and beauty—than any other scholar. For these reasons he incurred the venomous hatred of Pope, whose edition of Shakespeare he

had ventured to criticize, and who made 'peddling Tib-
balds' the hero of the earlier *Dunciad*, and succeeded
in covering his name with a cloud of obloquy, which
has only recently been dispelled by modern scholarship.[2]

The quarrel between Pope and Theobald started
that furious controversy about the text of Shakespeare
which raged with extreme violence for about a hundred
years, but which had the happy result of establishing
that standard and satisfactory text which is generally
accepted now.

IV

Still more important is the ascertainment, within
narrow limits, of the chronological order in which
Shakespeare wrote his plays. This immense discovery,
due to the accumulated labour through many years, of
many students, throws a great illumination upon Shakespeare's growth and the development of his powers. He
appears before us, no longer as an unnatural, full-blown
wonder, but as an artist like other artists, finding his
way step by step from promise to performance—from
bungling experiment to final achievement. Nor is there
indeed any artist in whom change and development are
more apparent—between whose early and whose later

[2] For the discreditable but fascinating story of Pope's treatment
of Theobald, see Professor Lounsbury's book, mentioned above,
p. 16. The Introduction to that great monument of Shakespearean
scholarship, the Cambridge *Shakespeare*, gives an authoritative account of the history of the text.

work there is a greater and more amazing contrast.

In the study of painting it has been found that the dating of a painter's pictures, and their chronological arrangement, not only provides a standpoint from which to view his work and study the growth of his gifts as an ordered whole, but also enables the art-researcher to detect in early work the foreshadowings of future achievement; the promise, before it has reached maturity, of what he has to give. In the same way, by the dating of Shakespeare's plays our modern conception of his total achievement is, in comparison with that of the eighteenth century, immensely clarified, deepened, and enriched. We have emerged at last into the daylight; we see the whole body of his plays, as Mr. Mackail has said, 'as an organic unity with continuous life, with diversity of operations, but one spirit.' 'He becomes solid and continuous: the planes come out, the lines of growth tell, the methods manifest themselves.'

When, therefore, I begin to read Shakespeare again, I pay no attention to the grotesque arrangement, taken from the Folio, of the plays, but follow the chronological order, which, with certain slight variations, is to be found in any handbook.[3]

My first reading is irresponsible and rapid, and is altogether delightful. How easy it is to read Shakespeare; why, I tell myself, there is nothing easier in

[3] Dowden's *Primer* (Macmillan), Masefield's little volume in the *Home University Library*, Chambers' *Survey*, Mr. John Bailey's recent book, or, in my opinion the best of all, Barrett Wendell's *William Shakespeare* (Scribner).

the world! All the great plays are obviously authentic;
almost all the great passages perfectly perspicuous, and
if they are not it doesn't seem to matter. Reading, as
Dr. Johnson advised, with total disregard of all the
commentators, I find that the barriers and bogeys disappear, the dangers which had terrified me fade away.
Passing over the plays written in his apprenticeship, I
begin with what was probably his first masterpiece and
real success, the *Midsummer Night's Dream*, written,
as it is generally supposed, about 1594.

> *Once I sat upon a promontory,*
> *And heard a mermaid on a dolphin's back*
> *Uttering such dulcet and harmonious breath,*
> *That the rude sea grew civil at her song,*
> *And certain stars shot madly from their spheres*
> *To hear the sea-maid's musick . . .*
> *That very time I saw, but thou couldst not,*
> *Flying between the cold moon and the earth,*
> *Cupid all arm'd: a certain aim he took*
> *At a fair vestal thronèd by the west,*
> *And loos'd his love-shaft smartly from his bow,*
> *As it should pierce a hundred thousand hearts;*
> *But I might see young Cupid's fiery shaft*
> *Quench'd in the chaste beams of the wat'ry moon,*
> *And the imperial votaress passed on,*
> *In maiden meditation, fancy-free.*
> *Yet mark'd I where the bolt of Cupid fell:*
> *It fell upon a little western flower,*
> *Before milk-white, now purple with love's wound,*
> *And maidens call it, Love-in-idleness.*

Who, the critics ask, was this mermaid on the
dolphin's back? Was she, as Warburton asserted,
Mary Queen of Scots, and the dolphin her husband,
the Dauphin and afterwards the King of France? Was
she literally seated on his back—which must have been
uncomfortable—or, as one critic suggests, merely 'back-
ing' and supporting him? Her 'dulcet and harmonious
breath'—does that describe her alluring Scottish accent;
and the stars that shot madly from their spheres to
listen to that accent—are these the English lords who
lost their heads, and lost them literally, in her cause?
The 'fair vestal throned by the west' was, all agree,
Queen Elizabeth, who quenched with her elderly and
chaste beams the fiery dart of Cupid. But who was this
young Cupid? Was he the Duke of Anjou, or the
middle-aged Earl of Leicester, and if so, was the 'little
western flower' Amy Robsart, or his third wife, Lettice
Knollys?

I do not try to solve these important problems, for
what is the meaning of a poem after all, but a pretext
for fine poetry? If that meaning be involved in haze,
may not the poetry be all the finer for it? So, above the
silvery mists of this *Dream* of the moon and midnight,
I float from mountain peak, as it were, to mountain
peak, to the three other great plays of this first period
(1594-1596)—*Romeo and Juliet, Richard II*, and *The
Merchant of Venice*. From the second period (1597-
1600) I pick out both the *Henry the Fourth* plays and

the three golden comedies—*Much Ado*, *Twelfth Night*, and *As You Like It*. From these I pass on to the seven great tragedies in their supposed order—*Julius Cæsar*, *Hamlet*, *Othello*, *Lear*, *Macbeth*, *Antony and Cleopatra*, *Coriolanus*, and with these read the tragic comedy, *Measure for Measure*. And then, of course, come *Cymbeline*, *The Winter's Tale* and *The Tempest*, those romances of his fourth and last period (1609-1612), after writing which he quietly returns home at the age of forty-eight to Stratford, having spent twenty profitable years in London—profitable to himself and to the world.

When, however, by this rapid, irresponsible survey I have again fixed in my mind the main features and great landmarks of this region, I find that I must retrace my steps for a more accurate and detailed exploration. I re-read the twenty great plays with more careful attention, and enrich my impressions by means of those interpretations of the great critics which I have mentioned, and which help me to observe all sorts of fascinating details which had escaped my observation.

v

An immense and learned history of Shakespearean criticism has recently been published.[4] These two great volumes are full of the profoundest interest and most

[4] *A History of Shakespearian Criticism*, by Augustus Ralli, 2 vols. Oxford Press, 1932.

intolerable boredom, and the record they contain is one which does no great credit to the intelligence of the human race.

Criticism, as Anatole France has said, is the latest in date of all literary forms; and though, as he adds, it may end in absorbing all the others, it has but slowly emerged from the Dead Sea of ancient theory, and succeeded, partially at least, in discriminating between esthetic and ethical considerations. The esthetic experience would appear indeed to be an extremely rare one; men, as Mr. Santayana says, are habitually insensible to beauty, and only in exceptional and scattered instances does she smile even on her adorers. Certainly the early criticism of Shakespeare, apart from the fine tributes of Ben Jonson and Dryden, and Milton's verses, is the saddest of sad stuff, the repetition of ancient formulas and the rattling of Aristotle's dry bones. But dimly we discern in it a faint awareness of the fact that Shakespeare was a great dramatist and poet; this impression, however, has to struggle hard against those buffeting east winds of doctrine which forced Ben Jonson and Dryden to qualify afterwards and almost retract their praises.

In the eighteenth century we observe the slow increase in this sense of awe and wonder, and note the full expression of it in one isolated little book, Maurice Morgann's *Essay on Falstaff;* and after that, the opinion that Shakespeare is the greatest of poets begins slowly to crystallize in England, although the deep-seated sorrow still persisted that he had no knowledge of the poetic art. And then at last the transcendental effulgence of Shakespeare's glory is unveiled by Goethe and the Germans, while Coleridge borrowed some at least of their fire, and claimed it as his own.

Once, however, the great principle was established that the critic's first duty is to experience beauty, and only after that to explain this experience to the intellect, and writers began in consequence to describe their concrete esthetic impressions—it was only then that the spectators and readers of Shakespeare's plays, who were for centuries so far ahead of the critics in genuine appreciation, began to lag quite as far behind them. By a whole series of fine critical interpretations Shakespeare was proved to be, when he wished—and he did generally wish it—atrocious as he is at times—the most consummate of all artists, and an almost unimaginably subtle writer, cunning, like Cleopatra, 'past man's thought,' and anyone possessed with the notion that he who runs may read will miss many of the most delicate touches of his art.

Thus, to give a few among many instances, I at least had never paid attention to the brief scene in *Measure for Measure* (II, iii), between Juliet and the Duke, until I read how Robert Bridges declared that even this short scene, 'where the Duke, graciously playing the confessor's rôle, finds himself at every professional move baffled and checkmated by the briefest possible replies of a loving, modest and true heart, till he is re-buffed into a Christlike sympathy, appears to me a masterpiece which, in its kind, no other dramatist can have equalled.' Another instance may be mentioned: a scene in the first part of *Henry IV* (II, i), of which Brandes writes:

'No sooner has the rebellion been hatched in the royal palace than the second act opens with a scene in an inn-yard on the Dover road. It is just daybreak; some carriers cross the yard with their lanterns, going to the stable to saddle their horses; they hail each other, gossip, and tell each other how they have passed the night. Not a word do they say about Prince Henry or Falstaff; they talk of the price of oats, and of how "This house is turned upside down since Robin Ostler died." Their speeches have nothing to do with the action: they merely sketch its locality and put the audience in tune for it; but seldom in poetry has so much been effected in so few words. The night sky, with Charles's wain "over the new chimney," the flickering gleam of the lanterns in the dirty yard, the fresh air of the early dawn, the misty atmosphere, the mingled odour of damp peas and beans, of bacon and ginger, all comes straight home to our senses. The situation takes hold of us with all the irresistible force of reality.'

I quote this passage as but one example among many of scenes in Shakespeare's most familiar masterpieces which a reader—at least a reader like myself—may easily overlook until his attention is called to their interest and significance.

VI

To take another instance. Few scenes in Shakespeare are more familiar to us than the opening scene of *Hamlet,* and yet the following analysis, which Dr. Furness quotes in his *Variorum* edition of the play (vol. II, p. 167), from an anonymous writer, gives to the first few lines of the play a new significance:

'The opening of *Hamlet,* this writer says, which is alive with excitement, striking contrasts, and the most delicate touches of nature, seems to have been taken by the editors, old and new, for nothing more than an unimpassioned conversation between two sentinels. Twice had Bernardo been encountered on the platform by the Ghost of the King, and he is now for the third time advancing at midnight to the scene of the apparition . . . In this state of mind he would be startled at every sight and sound . . . Thus alive to apprehension, he hears advancing footsteps; and the question, "Who's there?" is, to our ear, the sudden, instinctive exclamation of uncontrollable alarm, not the ordinary challenge between one sentinel and another . . . Francisco, the sentinel on duty, not recognizing a comrade in the terrified voice which hails him, replies "Nay, answer *me;* stand and unfold *yourself.*" But the moment Bernardo . . . calls out the watchword, "Long live the King!" in his habitual tones, does the sentinel know his *fellow* and greet him by his name.'

'You come most carefully upon your hour,' Francisco adds, and Bernardo, anxious to repel the notion that he is before his time, replies that the hour has struck, and dismisses the sentinel, whose reply, ' 'Tis bitter cold, and I am sick at heart,' suggests that in the contemplation of his own griefs he had not noticed Bernardo's ill-concealed agitation. And when Horatio and Marcellus appear, the latter, who had already seen the Ghost, shares Bernardo's excitement, and is unconscious of the presence of Francisco, and when Francisco bids him good night, he exclaims, like one awakened from a trance, 'O! farewell, honest soldier.'

In another of the most familiar and greatest scenes in Shakespeare, the death of Lear, Lamb calls attention to an exquisite touch which might easily escape the attention of the common reader. Just before his death, Lear half-recognizes Kent, his most devoted follower, and then forgets him. Some commentators have been shocked by Lear's seeming indifference; but this, Lamb says, 'is the magnanimity of authorship, when a writer, having a topic presented to him, fruitful of beauties for common minds, waives his privilege, and trusts to the judicious few for understanding the reason of his abstinence. What a pudder would a common dramatist have raised here of a reconciliation scene, a perfect recognition. . . . The old dying King partially catching at the truth, and immediately lapsing into obliviousness, with the high-minded carelessness of the other to have his services appreciated . . . are among the most judicious, not to say heart-touching strokes in Shakespeare.'

De Quincey's brief, famous essay *On the Knocking at the Gate in Macbeth*, is one of the great masterpieces of Shakespearean criticism, and should of itself be enough to convince any reader of how a fine piece of criticism can deepen and enrich our appreciation of a great work of art.

'From my boyish days,' De Quincey writes, 'I had always felt a great perplexity on one point in Macbeth. It was this: the knocking at the gate, which succeeds to the murder of Duncan, produced to my feelings an effect for which I never could account. The effect was, that it reflected back upon the murderer a peculiar awfulness and a depth of solemnity; yet, however obstinately I endeavoured with my understanding to comprehend this, for many years I never could see *why* it should produce such an effect.' In fact, his understanding told him positively that it could *not* produce any effect. 'But I knew better; I felt that it did; and I waited and clung to the problem until further knowledge should enable me to solve it.' This solution he found at last in one of the murders of the famous murderer, Williams, where the same incident, the knocking at the door soon after the murder was committed, which Shakespeare had invented, did actually occur,

and all the most eminent murder-dilettantes acknowl-
edged the felicity of the occurrence. Here De Quincey
found a fresh proof of how right he had been in rely-
ing on his own feeling in opposition to his understanding; it made him realize that a murder, when sympathy
is wholly felt with the murdered person, is in itself an
incident of coarse and vulgar horror; that, for the purposes of art, sympathy (in the proper sense of the word,
meaning comprehension of, and entering, into the feelings of another) must be with the murderer, not with
his victim. 'In the murderer, such a murderer as a poet
will condescend to, there must be raging some great
storm of passion—jealousy, ambition, vengeance, hatred
—which will create a hell within him; and into this hell
we are to look.'

But how could the transitory existence of this Hell,
replacing for a while the world of kindly human nature, with its elements of love and mercy, be most
vividly impressed upon us? Surely by its withdrawal;
just as when a person has fainted, the most affecting
moment, he tells his reader, is when a 'sigh and a stir-
ring announce the recommencement of suspended life.
Or, if the reader,' De Quincey adds, in one of the most
splendid passages of his splendid prose,

'has ever been present in a vast metropolis, on the day
when some great national idol was carried in funeral
pomp to his grave, and chancing to walk near the course
through which it passed, has felt powerfully in the

silence and desertion of the streets, and in the stagnation of ordinary business, the deep interest which at that moment was possessing the heart of man—if all at once he should hear the death-like stillness broken up by the sound of wheels rattling away from the scene, and making known that the transitory vision was dissolved, he will be aware that at no moment was his sense of the complete suspension and pause in ordinary human concerns so full and affecting, as at that moment when the suspension ceases, and the goings-on of human life are suddenly resumed. All action in any direction is best expounded, measured, and made apprehensible, by reaction. Now apply this to the case in *Macbeth*. Here, as I have said, the retiring of the human heart, and the entrance of the fiendish heart was to be expressed and made sensible. Another world has stept in; and the murderers are taken out of the region of human things, human purposes, human desires. They are transfigured: Lady Macbeth is "unsexed"; Macbeth has forgot that he was born of woman; both are conformed to the image of devils; and the world of devils is suddenly revealed. But how shall this be conveyed and made palpable? In order that a new world may step in, this world must for a time disappear. The murderers, and the murder must be insulated—cut off by an immeasurable gulf from the ordinary tide and succession of human affairs—locked up and sequestered in some deep recess; we must be made sensible that the world of ordinary life is suddenly arrested—laid asleep —tranced—racked into a dread armistice; time must be annihilated; relation to things without abolished; and all must pass self-withdrawn into a deep syncope and suspension of earthly passion. Hence it is, that when the deed is done, when the work of darkness is perfect, then the world of darkness passes away like a pageantry in the clouds: the knocking at the gate is heard; and it makes known audibly that the reaction has commenced; the human has made its reflux upon the fiendish; the pulses of life are beginning to beat again; and the re-establishment of the goings-on of the world in which we live, first makes us profoundly sensible of the awful parenthesis that had suspended them.'

I quote this passage at length, partly for the pleasure of copying out so fine a passage of English prose, and partly because I find in it an example of what criticism should be—the record first of all of an esthetic experience, vividly felt, though not comprehended, perhaps, by the reason, and then, with that reliance on his own feeling, even in opposition to his reason, which is the first duty of the true critic, the patient search for the explanation of the experience. and then its translation into terms of thought.[5]

VIII

Whether anyone had noticed before De Quincey the tremendous effect of this knocking on the gate I do not know, but it is not a great many years since that

[5] For another, and almost equally splendid essay on *Macbeth*, see Maeterlinck's preface to his translation of that play.

attention was first called to the awful effect of one of the most awful incidents in *Macbeth*—the sudden, silent appearance from nowhere, with no preparation, of that mysterious Third Murderer just before the death of Banquo (III, iii) who joins the two other assassins, and who cries, 'Hark! I hear horses,' as the victim draws near. Is this dark figure, as some believe, no other than Macbeth himself, or is he, as others hold, a supernatural appearance like the Witches, but more dreadful than the Witches—a horrible embodiment, in fact, of Murder itself, come to perpetrate those atrocities which the body of Banquo suffered, and which were more devilish than any that mere hirelings would be likely to inflict?

The existence of this mystery, which has been described as one of the greatest of the problems and mysteries in Shakespeare's plays, passed for long unnoticed; and even more extraordinary is the well-known fact that the problem of Hamlet's character was never remarked on till nearly at the end of the eighteenth century. The play was one of the most popular of Shakespeare's plays; nearly a score of writers mention Hamlet, and some of them write about him at length. But no one finds anything problematic or fascinating in him, or anything mysterious in his delay. He is regarded by the critics of the time as a gallant and romantic figure, the instrument, and at last the victim, of fate. Henry Mackenzie, the 'Man of Feeling,' was the first to write (in 1780) about the mystery and charm of Hamlet's character; but Goethe it was who called the world's attention to the problem of his delay. Before that date there was no Hamlet problem, but since then the character of Hamlet, as Dr. Bradley says, 'has probably exerted a greater fascination, and certainly has been the subject of more discussion, than any other in the whole literature of the world.' 'To pluck out,' as Browning phrased it, 'the heart of Hamlet's mystery'—how many have attempted this, though all have failed! [6]

IX

After these masterpieces, I read in their chronological order Shakespeare's first attempts, and his many pot-

[6] Of course they have failed, Professor Stoll explains. What could they do but fail?—there is absolutely no sign or smell of a mystery in Hamlet. Not only the play itself, but the unanimous testimony of the two centuries nearest to the playwright, prove, he repeats, that Hamlet is simply the brave and gallant hero of one of these revenge-plays of the classical and renascence stages. All the heroes of these must procrastinate; 'no delay, no play' is their predicament, and they must fill up the interval between the resolve and the deed as plausibly as they can; and this they do (he cites many instances) by self-reproaches, and usually too, like Hamlet, by feigning madness. If people would only study works of art in the light of other works of art, they would see that Hamlet's procrastination is due to nothing but the plot, and that when, after achieving his revenge he remarked, 'the rest is silence,' all he meant was that owing to his imminent decease, he hadn't time to tell his full story. In fact, our American professor adds, the modern morbid, psychological conception of Hamlet which has so obsessed Europe, that whole nations could say, as they did say, 'Germany is Hamlet!' 'Poland is Hamlet!' is an entirely false conception, and 'a blot on the intellectual record of our race.' See Professor Stoll's essay on *Hamlet*, mentioned above, p. 25.

boilers,[7] looking out for the splendid passages and scenes which are to be found in these. I read also the plays which are supposed to be only his in part,[7] listening for the sound of his great authentic voice breaking in upon the thin tinkle of his collaborators.[8]

In this second reading I read all the notes of some easily-handled and annotated edition—the *Arden* edition (Methuen), though the volumes are of unequal value, I find the best—and try to master the meaning of the obscure passages. But soon the madness is upon me; and I proceed still further in this adventure which has no end. My next plunge is into one immense volume after another of Dr. Furness's great *Variorum* edition (Lippincott). Here is a feast of reading enough

[7] Of the seventeen inferior plays of the Shakespeare canon, seven are the plays of his apprenticeship, *Titus Andronicus*, the three *Henry VI* plays, *Love's Labour's Lost*, the *Comedy of Errors*, and the *Two Gentlemen of Verona*. Three others, *The Taming of the Shrew*, *The Merry Wives of Windsor*, and *All's Well that Ends Well*, read like hack-work, and the historical plays, *Richard III*, *King John*, and *Henry V* may also be placed, perhaps, in this category; *Timon of Athens* seems to be only partly Shakespeare's, and *Pericles* and *Henry VIII* were obviously written in collaboration. *Troilus and Cressida*, though plainly written by Shakespeare, is, in spite of the splendid passages, a most unpleasant play.

[8] The most famous instance of this occurs at the beginning of the third act of *Pericles*, where, after such doggerel lines as

> *So up and down the poor ship drives,*
> *The lady shrieks, and well a-near*
> *Does fall in travail with her fear,*

'the full swell' (I quote Mr. Mackail) 'of the incomparable Shakespearean verse breaks on us with "Thou God of this great vast, rebuke these surges".' There is no thrill in the whole of Shake-to fill a lifetime—the accumulated essays and interpretations and controversies of hundreds of past critics. I find of the utmost fascination these ponderous volumes, where a few lines of the text hardly raise their heads above the mad seas of comment at their base; and where often a single phrase is followed by page after page in which critics fly at each other's throats. Dr. Furness accumulates these records of wild absurdity; and then raising his head like Neptune, with his own calm wisdom, rebukes these surges. Here also one can bewilder one's reason with the great insoluble cruxes of the Shakespearean text—the 'dram of eale,' the 'drink up eisel,' the 'good kissing carrion' of Hamlet, the 'runaway's eyes' of Juliet; and believe, and then disbelieve,

---

speare, this fine critic says, that is greater than what we feel when we suddenly hear this voice. Then also there are the plays falsely ascribed to Shakespeare, which Professor Tucker Brooke has collected in his admirable *Shakespeare Apocrypha* (Oxford Press)— another book that all Shakespeare readers should possess. When we look for gleams of Shakespeare among these spurious plays, the same thrills may stir us, and they are all the more thrilling because we cannot be sure that they are his. I like to think that Shakespeare wrote, in *The Two Noble Kinsmen*, Emilia's prayer to Diana:

> O sacred, shadowy, cold and constant Queen,
> Abandoner of revels, mute, contemplative,

and I am certain of Shakespeare's autograph in Arcite's invocation to the God of War:

> O Great Corrector of enormous times,
> Shaker of o'er-rank states, thou grand decider
> Of dusty and old titles, that heal'st with blood
> The earth when it is sick, and cur'st the world
> O' th' pleurisy of people.

and then believe again in Theobald's perfect, but perhaps too perfect, 'babbled of green fields.' [9]

[9] For the story of this most famous of all Shakespearean emendations, from 'a Table of green fields,' to 'a' babbled of green fields,' see Professor Lounsbury's book (mentioned above, p. 16), pp. 161-168.

There are certain other felicitous emendations in the text of Shakespeare which our more modern and austere criticism rejects, but which I wish it had had the unscrupulous magnanimity to retain.

If Shakespeare did not write these suggested words, he certainly ought to have written them; as, for instance, when Cleopatra exclaims,

> *O Sun!*
> *Burn the great sphere thou mov'st in; darkling stand*
> *The varying shore o' the world.*
>
> (*A. & C.*, IV, xiii.)

I would go to the stake for it that what Cleopatra said was *star*, as Staunton suggested in 1873—'The varying star o' the world,' what a phrase for the changing moon!—and not the *shore* of the original text, which is variously explained as meaning the whole earth where light and darkness made an incessant variation (Warburton), or the *orbis terrarum*, with its irregular outline, and deeply-indented shores (Furness). The Cambridge editors and the *Arden* Shakespeare reject this beautiful emendation, but the *Oxford Shakespeare* prints *star*.

When in the opening lines of *Twelfth Night* the love-sick Duke exclaims,

> *That strain again! It had a dying fall:*
> *O! it came o'er my ear like the sweet* sound
> *That breathes upon a bank of violets,*

I am enchanted by Pope's emendation of *south* for the Folio's *sound*, to explain which Dr. Furness devotes three closely-printed pages. This emendation, which was adopted by Theobald, and which retained its place in the text without question for more than a hundred years, has now been rejected by the Oxford and Cambridge editors and all modern scholars, but I am loath to give it up.

In the phrase of the Host of the Garter Inn in *The Merry Wives*, when he engages Bardolph as a tapster, 'Let me see thee froth and *live*' (I, iii), the word *live*, though in the Folios and the third Quarto, has since Capell been rejected for the prosaic word *lime*, of the first two Quartos, meaning 'to put lime into liquor.' But 'let me see thee froth and live,'—what a phrase for Bardolph, and for many people one knows!

But the attempt to improve the poetry of great poets, though one of the most fascinating, is certainly the most wanton and impudent of literary pastimes. I never do it.

THE GREAT REWARD

I. POETRY

Chapter III

THE GREAT REWARD

I. POETRY

N ow that I have returned from the journey into Shakespeare's world, this plunge into the sea of books which surrounds that world, I feel impelled, like other travellers and voyagers, to exhibit the spoils I have brought back with me. No one, it has been said, should write about Shakespeare without a special licence; but although I do not hope to procure any such licence from the pundits, I cannot resist the temptation to describe the impression which this adventure has left upon me. I shall at least clarify my own experience; and my unlicensed essay may be of use to other unprofessional readers like myself. Many people, as it has been said, read in Shakespeare, but few really read him; but I at least have performed this feat.

To anyone who reads the works of Shakespeare in their chronological order, from 1592, when at the age of twenty-eight he began, as far as we know for certain, to write, till the date (1607) of *Antony and Cleopatra* (for after this date his five remaining years of authorship show a certain decline, amidst all their splendour)—to any such reader the first impression must be that he has watched a growth of genius more astounding than any other which the world ever witnessed. In this supreme period of fifteen years—and Sainte-Beuve has defined the span of fifteen years as the period in the life of a great genius during which he produces his greatest work—in this brief period Shakespeare rises like a Jinn from a bottle till he seems to fill the sky. His early compositions, though written at an age older than the age at which Keats and Shelley had produced so much of their finest work, betray no signs of overwhelming power. The two long poems, composed when he was nearly thirty—that 'couple of ice-houses,' as Hazlitt called them, are pedantic studies of lust, without the least evidence of a dramatic gift—they are samples of good, sound, but uninspired Elizabethan verse. Yet two signs of power they do reveal: first of all that rich sensuousness and, indeed, sensuality which is almost a necessary part of great artistic endowment and with which no art, as Goethe said, can afford to dispense;— and with this, and due, no doubt, to it, a richness and concreteness of imagery and sense-impressions. A sensuous love of words they also show, and a meticulous care in the choice of phrases, a love of literary polish, and a laborious effort to acquire that mastery of language, which, to the artist whose medium of expression it is, must be the first and most essential endowment—or acquirement—of all.

II

There are two main methods of attaining excellence in writing, two ways of attempting to reach the peaks of Parnassus. The poet may attempt to fly thither on the wings of meaning, hoping that his high thoughts will float him aloft; or he may, step by step, cut his way thither with toil and labour. He may—to change the metaphor—begin by pressing out from life and experience the juice of meaning, and then find a receptacle to hold it; or the goldsmith's art may be his first preoccupation: he may carve and chisel and adorn his work with jewels, till at last the wine of imaginative meaning begins to fill the empty, elaborated cup. Shakespeare's early work shows that this latter method was his method. At the age of thirty he was still a euphuist, a lover of words for the sake of words, delighting in their sounds and rhymes and overtones, in 'taffeta phrases, silken terms precise,' and, like Armado in his early play,

> *One whom the music of his own vain tongue*
> *Doth ravish like enchanting harmony.*

Of all that wealth of poetic emotion seeking to find expression, that mass of brooding thought we are aware of in the work of young poets like Shelley and Keats, there is no trace; we find at first in Shakespeare little more than a delight in verbal experiment and an unusual sensibility to the expressive and musical qualities of words.

Once, and once only in the history of a people, there comes a divine moment when its speech seems to those who write it a new-found wonder; when its language is in a plastic state, unstereotyped and unhackneyed; and it is at this moment that the one supreme poet, the Homer, the Dante, the Shakespeare, appears; for no form of speech seems rich enough to provide material for more than a single poet of this rank.

And what material as yet unexploited for literary purposes Shakespeare found ready at his hand! There were the learned vocabularies of the law and of theology, both of which he freely pillaged; there was the vigorous speech, full of wit and repartee and vituperation of the townsmen, innkeepers, shopkeepers, tradesmen of Stratford and of London; and beneath this the living talk of the countryside and the dialects of uplandish people, full of coarseness, and full also of the beautiful unconscious poetry of rustic speech, images and magical descriptive words and fresh country flowers with the breath of spring and the dew of the morning on them.

Shakespeare's plays, as Sir Walter Raleigh has said, are extraordinarily rich in the floating debris of popular proverbs, sayings, scraps and tags and broken ends of speech and song, caught out of the air or picked up by the roadside; and all this illiterate material he turned to the most exquisite literary use.

And then, in addition to these rich native sources, many wonderful new words were flooding into England from foreign lands; far-fetched, strange, exotic terms like *alligator, cannibal* and *hurricano,* and many others, brought home by English sailors and English pirates from the East and the West Indias, from Mexico and South America; and those aureate Italian words, imported into England by young Italianate travellers of fashion, words like *Paragon, Artist, Sonnet, Stanza, Madrigal, Conversation, Cavalier, Courtezan* and *Duello.*

III

But the passionate word-hunters of the time were not only collectors, but inventors as well. In addition to their generous hospitality, their willingness to welcome any of those terms 'of magnificence and splendour,' which, as Dryden later said, must be imported from abroad, they were equally ready to experiment freely with native words, to try anything with them and see what happened, to make compounds of them, derivatives from them, to form verbs from nouns, and nouns from verbs and adjectives. In that age of complete linguistic freedom and experimental gusto the making of words became the sport of sports among the young intellectuals of fashion. How they created and coined and fantasticated them to please their fancy, made them ring and sing and rhyme together without a thought whether reason had any hand in the matter! In Shakespeare's early comedy, *Love's Labour's Lost*, we find, as Mr. Gordon has said, the playground of the new language.

I know of no better description of the English of the time than that of Dr. Abbott:

'for freedom, for brevity and for vigour, Elizabethan is superior to modern English. Many of the words employed by Shakespeare and his contemporaries were the recent inventions of the age; hence they were used with a freshness and exactness to which we are strangers. Again, the spoken English so far predominated over the grammatical English that it materially influenced the rhythm of the verse, the construction of the sentence, and even sometimes the spelling of words. Hence sprung an artless and unlaboured harmony which seems the natural heritage of Elizabethan poets, whereas such harmony as is attained by modern authors frequently betrays a painful excess of art. Lastly, the use of some few still remaining inflections (the subjunctive in particular), the lingering *sense* of many other inflections that had passed away leaving behind something of the old versatility and audacity in the arrangement of the sentence, the stern subordination of grammar to terseness and clearness, and the consequent directness and naturalness of expression, all conspire to give a liveliness and wakefulness to Shakespearian English which are wanting in the grammatical monotony of the present day. We may perhaps claim some superiority in completeness and perspicuity for modern English, but if we were to appeal on this ground to the shade of Shakespeare in the words of Antonio in the *Tempest*,—

> *Do you not hear us speak?*

we might fairly be crushed with the reply of Sebastian—

> *I do; and surely*
> *It is a sleepy language.'* [1]

IV

Into this wild ocean of words Shakespeare plunged head over heels, and disported himself in it with a wild dolphin joy. He collected words from everywhere, from rustic speech and dialect (he no doubt spoke the Warwickshire dialect all his life), from Chaucer and old books, from translators of the classics, from lawyers and grave theologians, from travelled young gallants. He was, moreover, perhaps the greatest word-creator the world has ever known, and has probably added more new words to our vocabulary than all the other English poets put together. He made up his language as he went along—'crashing,' as he has been described, 'through the forest of words like a thunderbolt, crushing them out of shape if they don't fit in, melting moods and tenses, and leaving people to gape at the transformation.'

And yet he was by no means a word-eccentric like his contemporaries, Harvey and Chapman and Nashe,

[1] A *Shakespearian Grammar*, E. A. Abbott (Macmillan).

those magpies in their passion for odds and ends of language; he did not, like Spenser, make for himself a precious form of speech for his private use; he was no Anarch in this world of anarchy, but in the midst of the linguistic chaos of his time created a Paradise for the English-speaking race. His instinct for acceptable terms which might become current coin was unusually sure, and, as Mr. Gordon says, his sensitiveness 'to the quality, the habits, and the history of the words he played with was a trained gift.' And Shakespeare possessed an even rarer gift, which can be best described by another quotation from Mr. George Gordon's little masterpiece, *Shakespeare's English*,[2] his genius, namely, in the manipulation and development of meaning.

'It is exercised with habitual felicity on the commonest expressions in the language, and is an abstract of that shaping power exerted daily and almost unconsciously by every nation of speakers. The miracle is to see so communal an engine in private hands. Shakespeare possessed this power in a degree never approached before or since by any Englishman, or perhaps by any individual mind; he seems, as he employs it, to be doing the work of a whole people.'

Thus Shakespeare became, as I have said, the great Lord of Language, the most expressive, the most articulate of human beings.

What words or tongue of Seraph can suffice?

[2] *S.P.E. Tract No. XXIX*, Oxford Press, 1928.

Raphael replied to Adam when our first parent asked that Archangel to recount the mighty record of God's creation of the world; and indeed, if ever there was a tongue which could suffice to tell of the wonders of this created world, that Seraph's tongue was Shakespeare's. He could say anything that could be said, describe both Nature and all its mighty works and clothe man's subtlest thoughts in the most transparent and luminous raiment of perfect expression.[3]

Shakespeare added, not only more words, but more figurative and proverbial phrases to our speech, than any other author has ever added to any language.[4] He may be regarded as being one of the great creators of the English language, and certainly it is owing to him that English, which till the end of the seventeenth century was almost unknown and never read abroad, has become a second speech to several other races; nor is it hardly an exaggeration to say, as a Shakespeare enthusiast has said, that 'through his greatness a Low Dutch dialect has become the chiefest instrument of civilization, the world-speech of humanity at large.'[5]

[3] 'There has never been a writer,' as Sir Walter Raleigh says, 'who came nearer to giving adequate verbal expression to the subtlest turns of consciousness, the flitting shadows and half-conceived ideas and purposes which count for so much in the life of the mind.' (*Shakespeare*, p. 216.)

[4] I give a list of about one hundred of these in my *Words and Idioms*, pp. 227-228.

[5] *The Man Shakespeare*, Frank Harris, p. xix.

V

And yet it is curious to note that the supremest gift of language, that gift of the magic and evocatory phrase, which has made Shakespeare the master-magician of the world, was by no means, with him, as with many young poets, a natural endowment; and we find few traces of it in the long poems he so carefully composed when nearly thirty. His earliest plays are written in the common poetic diction of his time—that style of the day which, as Swinburne says, all great poets begin by writing, and lesser poets write all their lives. In the earlier historical plays, where Shakespeare's authorship is disputed, it is hardly possible to discriminate by any criterion of style which parts are of his composition. In the powerful rhetoric and plangent declamation of certain passages in these plays we seem to be first aware of Shakespeare's gift of language; but it is only in the *Two Gentlemen of Verona*, with the song 'Who is Silvia,' with the line:

The uncertain glory of an April day,

and the passage about the brook that makes sweet music as it strays, that his power over words becomes a magic power, and his golden mastery of speech begins to almost blind us with its beauty.

Emerson describes how he once went to see the Hamlet of a famous actor, and how all that he remembered of this great tragedian was simply his question to the Ghost:

> *What may this mean,*
> *That thou, dead corse, again in complete steel*
> *Revisit'st thus the glimpses of the moon?*

This enchanted radiance of language, which for Emerson blotted out the stage, the actor and the drama, is for some spectators or readers of Shakespeare's plays the most potent spell which they cast upon him. Of *Troilus and Cressida* they will remember the lines:

> *I stalk about her door,*
> *Like a strange soul upon the Stygian banks*
> *Staying for waftage.*

Or from *Timon:*

> *Lie where the light foam of the sea may beat*
> *Thy grave-stone daily.*

And even in that appalling play of beastly horror, *Titus Andronicus*, when the wretched Lavinia enters, 'ravished,' according to the stage-directions, 'her hands cut off, and her tongue cut out,' her uncle Marcus speaks of the villain who has mutilated her in a phrase 'by all the Muses filed':

> *O! had the monster seen those lily hands*
> *Tremble, like aspen leaves, upon a lute!*

It may almost seem to such word-intoxicated readers as if Shakespeare sometimes used his plays merely for

the opportunities they gave him for this lyric utterance;
he turns the martial Othello and the savage Macbeth
into supreme poets; he places, however incongruously,
great verse in the mouth of any prosaic character who
happens to be at hand, like Queen Gertrude's aria on
Ophelia's death, or those lines of dark magic which he
makes the thin lips of Iago utter:

> *Not poppy, nor mandragora,*
> *Nor all the drowsy syrops of the world.*

And what poetry he puts into the mouths of his murderers!

> *Their lips were four red roses on a stalk,*
> *Which in their summer beauty kiss'd each other,*

Forrest says, after his and Dighton's 'ruthless butchery'
of the Princes in the Tower (*R. III*, IV, iii); and it is
the first murderer in *Macbeth*, who, while they are
waiting to slaughter Banquo, poetically remarks,

> *The west yet glimmers with some streaks of day:*
> *Now spurs the lated traveller apace*
> *To gain the timely inn.* (III, iii)

So too in enchanting words the savage Caliban describes the Enchanted Island to the drunken sailors:

> *Be not afeard: the isle is full of noises,*
> *Sounds and sweet airs, that give delight, and hurt not.*
> *Sometimes a thousand twangling instruments*
> *Will hum about mine ears; and sometimes voices,*
> *That, if I then had wak'd after long sleep,*

Will make me sleep again: and then, in dreaming,
The clouds methought would open and show riches
Ready to drop upon me; that, when I wak'd
I cried to dream again. (Tempest, III, ii)

Even on the face of the Professor in Minnesota we detect a smile; his lips, like the lips at sunrise of the great statue of Memnon, are touched with music as he speaks of the splendour of Shakespeare's poetry, 'shed' as he describes it 'like the rain and the light of heaven, on the just and the unjust.'

VI

This splendour of poetry—and Shakespeare, if not the most correct, is the most opulent and most magical of all poets—was the first of his genial gifts which reached maturity, and which in the *Two Gentlemen* and the plays of about that date makes its first shining appearance, flashes up, in *A Midsummer Night's Dream,* like a flood from an inexhaustible fountain. Of the great poetry in the other great lyrical plays of this period, in *Romeo and Juliet,* in the *Merchant of Venice,* and in *Richard II,* and in the three Golden Comedies which followed, I need not speak; this middle style of Shakespeare's poetry, could it be imitated, would be the most perfect model and absolute pattern of what poetry should be. But it cannot be imitated: unlike Æschylus or Virgil or Dante or Milton, Shakespeare has no mannerisms: we recognize his lines only by their supreme felicity, their 'effortless power,' as it has been well described, 'and their incomparable sweetness.'

And yet there is one quality or characteristic of Shakespeare's poetry which, though it cannot be imitated, distinguishes it from that of all other poets. This quality is his possession, in a supreme degree, of the greatest of all poetic gifts, a sensuous, pictorial imagination, and the power of embodying his thoughts in images of beauty and splendour. 'Every word,' as Gray said of him, 'is a picture'; and these pictures often flash from the length of a line or phrase with the quickness of lightning-flashes. This unparalleled wealth of imagery shows itself, above all, in that royal use of metaphor, which is the most distinguishing quality of his style, and which Aristotle described as the surest mark of genius. 'He could not speak but a figure came.' His thought passes from metaphor to metaphor, each of them bringing a glint of colour and suggestion, and forming an iridescent, or a dark and shadowy, background to the scenes depicted. These metaphors he draws from every source, from trees, from flowers, from the sea and clouds, and seasons, and from the simplest, humblest things of the house or farm, from domestic animals, cats and dogs, or from the nobler creatures of the wild, from eagles, deer and lions or fierce tigers, and above all from the features and movements of the human body. He even brings to life the half-obliterated images of popular idiom, each with a figure or action, a shade of feeling of its own, which, as Maeterlinck pointed out, no translator is able to translate to another language.

Shakespeare does not confine himself, like many poets, only to visual images; he makes use of impressions from the other senses, the senses of smell and hearing; and seems to have been especially fond of images of reverberating sound, trumpets and horns and the baying of hounds echoing from afar. Motor images as they are called, sensations of effort, strain, movement, of rushing winds or horses, are frequent in his poetry, and also of the tides and the surges of the sea ('surge' is a favourite word with Shakespeare) and of the flow of rivers, as in one of his most splendid images, of the Pontic sea:

> *Whose icy current and compulsive course*
> *Ne'er feels retiring ebb, but keeps due on*
> *To the Propontic and the Hellespont.*

VII

Shakespeare uses his images, his similes and metaphors, at first in the manner of Spenser and most other poets, as decorations and adornments of his verse. When for instance, Romeo, in his early play, sees Juliet at the window and exclaims:

> *It is the east, and Juliet is the sun!*
> *Arise, fair sun, and kill the envious moon,*
> *Who is already sick and pale with grief.*

These images, and those that follow about the moon's vestal livery and Juliet's eyes twinkling like stars in heaven, are pure decoration, and very pretty and conceited decoration they make. But as Shakespeare grows in poetic power, he employs his images, not only for ornament, but for far higher purposes; his metaphors, transmuted in his imagination, interpret and in a sense create the life he depicts. Of this kind of creative imagery he becomes with Æschylus a supreme master. If we read again the familiar passage in *Macbeth:*

> *Tomorrow, and tomorrow, and tomorrow,*
> *Creeps in this petty pace from day to day,*
> *To the last syllable of recorded time;*
> *And all our yesterdays have lighted fools*
> *The way to dusty death. Out, out, brief candle!*
> *Life's but a walking shadow, a poor player*
> *That struts and frets his hour upon the stage,*
> *And then is heard no more; it is a tale*
> *Told by an idiot, full of sound and fury,*
> *Signifying nothing,*

we cannot but see how such images in this supremely imaginative passage, whether visual,—'lighted,' and 'brief candle'; or audible,—'syllable,' 'heard no more,' 'sound and fury';—or the motor images,—'creeps,' 'walking shadow,' 'struts and frets'—are no mere decorations; and in general we may say that the great Shakespearean characters, like primitive man, create what they express by clothing their ideas in images.

But Shakespeare uses his metaphors in a still more subtle and sublime fashion. Maeterlinck, in his Preface to his translation of *Macbeth*, notes how the deep impression which this play makes upon us is due to the images which swarm in the speeches of the characters, who thus make the atmosphere they breathe, and who become in turn the tragic creatures of that atmosphere. It is the innumerable stir and whisper of these images, he says, which give its inner and profound life to *Macbeth*; and though we are hardly conscious of them, they are the cause of the inexplicable power of the play upon us.

This special tone or atmosphere in *Macbeth* is described by Dr. Bradley as being due, in part at least, to the frequent occurrence of images of darkness and night, or rather of black night broken by flashes of light and colour; and that colour was especially the colour of blood.[6]

'Blood, Blood, Blood!' these dreadful images, these awful metaphors, keep muttering 'Blood' in a kind of undersong all through the play. Macbeth sees gouts of blood on the imaginary dagger before Duncan's murder; blood on his own hands afterwards, blood that not all the green ocean could wash away, but would rather stain the multitudinous sea with red; he invokes the

[6] *Shakespearean Tragedy*, p. 335.

'bloody and invisible' hand of night before Banquo's murder; 'there's blood upon thy face!' he whispers to the murderer at the banquet afterwards, and says, 'Never shake thy gory locks at me!' to the ghost of Banquo.

It will have blood, they say; blood will have blood,

he cries, when the guests have departed; and in the cavern scene, where the apparition of 'a bloody child' bids him 'be bloody, bold, and resolute,' still the blood-boltered Banquo smiles in awful derision upon him.

Lady Macbeth too is haunted by images of blood; cannot wash the smell of it from her hand; while Malcolm and Macduff in England lament the bleeding of their country under the 'bloody-scepter'd tyrant'; and Lennox prays for feasts and banquets freed from 'bloody knives'; and as Macbeth's enemies approach Dunsinane, one of them describes his deeds in what is perhaps the most terrible metaphor of the play; terrible, because blood is suggested by its texture, but is not named:

Now does he feel
His secret murders sticking on his hands.

I quote from Dr. Caroline Spurgeon, who has carried much further the suggestion of the reiteration of images in Shakespeare's plays, her hypothesis being that not only *Macbeth,* but each of the great tragedies has a dominating image, or set of images, which, like a floating picture, or under-song of recurrent themes and *motivs* in music, gives to each its special tone, atmosphere and colour. The tragedy of *Romeo and Juliet*, for instance, is full of images of light, the flash of brilliant light quenched suddenly in darkness. Out of candle-light, torches, the sparkle of fire, the flash of powder, and especially of bright or evil stars, Shakespeare forms, for the story of these 'star-crossed' lovers, and their love—too quick, too quickly quenched—'too like the lightning,' as Juliet herself describes it, or in the Friar's words:

> *Like fire and powder,*
> *Which as they kiss consume—*

out of these he forms, Dr. Spurgeon writes, 'a continuous and consistent running image of exquisite beauty, building up a definite picture and atmosphere of brilliance swiftly quenched, which powerfully affects the imagination of the reader.'

The dominating metaphors in *Hamlet*, she says, are images of illness and disease, of some tumour, a hidden rank corruption, which, 'mining all within, infects unseen.'

The atmosphere of space and magnitude which surrounds the figures in *Antony and Cleopatra*, is created, she adds, by recurring images of great elemental forces, of the wide world, of the sun and moon and the sea and sky and vastness generally; of that 'demi-Atlas of the earth,' Antony, who was willing to let, for Cleopatra's love, 'the wide arch of the ranged empire' fall;

so that, when this giant fell himself, his paramour could find

> *Nothing left remarkable*
> *Beneath the visiting moon.*[7]

It was, however, not these great qualities that charmed Shakespeare's contemporaries, but the 'honey-tongued sweetness' of his wood-notes wild; this is the quality of his verse they always notice; and surely for us, at least this blackbird's fluting, and the divine airs which he, like Mozart, seems to have caught from heaven, can never lose, any more than the blackbird's song or Mozart's music can lose, their enchantment, even in our disenchanted ears.

The Merchant of Venice is not for many lovers of Shakespeare one of their favourite plays. Its theatricality and stage-effectiveness put a cheat upon them which they afterwards resent. But the other day, when I happened to look into it—'The moon shines bright'— these first words of the last Act put a kind of magic on me:

> *In such a night as this,*
> *When the sweet wind did gently kiss the trees*
> *And they did make no noise,—*

---

[7] Dr. Spurgeon has made a prolonged study of Shakespeare's images, the results of which she promises to give before long to the world. So far she has published only two fascinating but most tantalising foretastes of the feast she promises: a pamphlet (from which I have quoted above) of the Shakespeare Association entitled, *Leading Motives in the Imagery of Shakespeare's Tragedies* (Oxford Press, 1930), and *Shakespeare's Iterative Imagery*, British Academy Lecture, 1931 (Oxford Press).

In such a night
Stood Dido with a willow in her hand
Upon the wild sea banks, and waft her love
To come again to Carthage,—

when Lorenzo and Jessica were out-nighting each
other in such a night as this, what could I do but revel
in the moonlight and enchanted echoes of this scene?

Sit, Jessica: look, how the floor of heaven
Is thick inlaid with patines of bright gold:
There's not the smallest orb which thou behold'st
But in his motion like an angel sings,
Still quiring to the young-eyed cherubins;
Such harmony is in immortal souls;
But, whilst this muddy vesture of decay
Doth grossly close it in, we cannot hear it.

Poetry was given to man, Goethe said, to make him
satisfied with himself and with his lot. Certainly for me
poetry, either in verse or prose, exquisitely performs
this function. I may be old and cross and ill, a wasted
life may lie behind me, and the grave yawn close in
front. I may have lost my faith, my illusions, my teeth,
my reputation and umbrella. What does it matter? It
doesn't matter in the least! Reading Lorenzo's words,

Come, ho! and wake Diana with a hymn!

off I go into the enchanted forest, into the Age of Gold.
Life ceases to be brief, sad, enigmatic; I am perfectly
satisfied with it. What more is there indeed to ask for?

I taste a joy beyond the reach of fate; *le bonheur, l'impossible bonheur,* is mine. I am (to express myself in soberer terms) simply kidnapped into heaven. I sit with the Gods and quaff their nectar; quaff indeed a nectar more generous than their own, since I, alone of the Immortals, taste the aroma of this aromatic, floating orchard plot of earth, which, could they but sip its fragrance, how gladly would the Gods descend from their golden chairs, take upon themselves the burden of our earthly sin, and provoke another Flood! Even that 'fading mansion,' my aching, coughing body, becomes a vehicle and instrument of music, and like a battered old violin, shivers and vibrates with tunable delight. 'Therefore the poet,' as Lorenzo went on to tell Jessica,

Did feign that Orpheus drew trees, stones, and flood;
Since naught so stockish, hard, and full of rage,
But music for the time doth change his nature.

If ever again I am so stockish or full of rage as to deny the genius of Shakespeare, the music of this scene will, in the magical five minutes it takes to read it through, charm me back from my backsliding.

By the time he had written *Hamlet* it would seem as if Shakespeare had reached perfection as a poet: as if the mastery of the art of language could be carried no further point. But as we watch the onrush of his genius, one of the things which almost takes our breath is the way he will leap beyond what seems perfection

to heights above anything we could have possibly imagined. After *Hamlet*, the sweet perfection of his verse
is more and more replaced by a more vehement and
vaster music, and by passages illuminated, as by flashes
of lightning, with phrases of supreme simplicity, but of
supreme sublimity, in which the meaning is no longer
set, as it were, to the music and patterned to the rhythm
of his verse, but creates its own rhythm and is the very
essence of that rhythm—a few words which, transcend-
ing all rhetoric and poetry, illuminate the darkness of
some tragic situation and carry with them an unequalled
sense of strangeness and an almost intolerable poign-
ancy.

It is the cause, it is the cause, my soul—

Tomorrow, and tomorrow, and tomorrow—

The long day's task is done,
And we must sleep.

My heart dances;
But not for joy; not joy—

No, no, no life!—

Thou'lt come no more,
Never, never, never, never, never!

There are poets, it may be, who have written poetry
as great, or nearly as great as that of Shakespeare, but
no poet has ever approached sublimity like this; this
beauty beyond beauty belongs to him alone—in the
circle of that great magic none dare walk but he.

THE GREAT REWARD

II. CHARACTER

Chapter IV

THE GREAT REWARD

II. CHARACTER

THIS unprecedented mastery of language is, then, the first of Shakespeare's gifts whose swift development we are aware of as we follow the sequence of his works. But following close upon this gift of poetic evocation we begin to be aware of another and even more astounding evocatory power— of something which is almost new in the history of literature, something which is far beyond our analysis, but which we can observe in the effect that, as play follows play, it more and more amazingly produces.

The drama has an ancient history, and it had produced great masterpieces long before Shakespeare. These masterpieces are, of course, the masterpieces of the Greek drama; but of more influence in the time of Elizabeth were the tragedies of Seneca, which were so much studied and imitated in that age. The personages who figure in the Greek and Roman plays, and in the plays of Shakespeare's contemporaries, are all more or less stage-characters, personages demanded by the situation, the embodiments of humours and passions, or merely mouth-pieces through which the playwright speaks. They are, indeed, often ideal types and noble inventions, but they have no life of their own apart from the play in which they figure; when that is over, they cease to exist; they are puppets, if sublime puppets, to be put away in the box from which their inventor took them.

Marlowe and Ben Jonson accepted this classical conception of human nature as being composed of typical forms, with one dominant trait thrown into high relief; their personages are no more than their labels imply: they never outrun the requirements of the plays in which they appear, and they act up to their descriptions in all circumstances. Such, indeed, are almost all the personages in our modern drama; and, as Mr. Desmond MacCarthy has said of the characters in the plays of Mr. Bernard Shaw, 'we know exactly how they would behave in connections which exhibit their classifiable characteristics, but apart from contacts which bring these out, they disappear from view as human beings.' 'They go,' to borrow a phrase from the same critic, 'the way of all waxworks.'

The characters in the plays of Shakespeare's earliest period are of this description; they are stage dummies, and the embodiments of single qualities and simple forces. Analysis, as Swinburne says, would be inapplicable to them for there is nothing in them that we can analyse.

But after Shakespeare's earliest attempts at drama an odd thing happens on the stage. Now and then, among the attendants of the great stage dummies, a humble

figure comes to life; an eye catches our eye, we hear
the sound of a living voice, and the sense of the theatre
is replaced for a moment by the illusion of reality.
These real people appear at first in scenes which are,
for the most part, of no importance; they are but em-
bryos and are presented sketchily at first, like Launce
and Speed in the *Two Gentlemen of Verona*, and the
Host in that play, which, hiding with Julia as she woe-
fully listens to her false lover declare his love to her
rival, suddenly awakes with the exclamation: 'By my
halidom, I was fast asleep.' Almost the earliest [1] of
these figures who becomes a living being is the preposterous weaver Bottom; soon after him Juliet's nurse
rushes upon the stage and fills the scenes in which she
appears with her full-blown and outrageous vitality.[2]
She is the first of that great rout of Shakespeare's un-
seemly disreputables who form so potent a rabble in
his plays.

Shakespeare was always an experimenter; and it

[1] Mr. Granville-Barker has, however, pointed out how, in less
than forty words, Costard, in *Love's Labour's Lost*, transforms the
poor country curate, Sir Nathaniel (who has broken down in his
attempt to act the part of Alexander the Great in the masque)
from a stage-puppet into a human being—and comes himself alive
in the process—when he describes him as 'a foolish mild man; an
honest man, look you, and soon dashed! He is a marvellous good
neighbour, faith, and a very good bowler; but, for Alisander,—
alas, you see how 'tis,—a little o'erparted' (V, ii).

[2] 'The nurse . . . is a triumphant and complete achievement.
She stands four-square, and lives and breathes in her own right. . . .
He will give us nothing completer till he gives us Falstaff' (Gran-
ville-Barker, *Prefaces*, II, 42).

seems to have occurred to him quite early that it would be amusing, and perhaps dramatically effective, to place his stage figures, whose rhetorical encounters it was his business to dramatize, against a background touched here and there by gleams of real life as his audience knew it. This theatrical experiment may have been suggested to him by the old Morality Plays, with their realistic scenes of contemporary life. The innovation was, no doubt, a success from the very beginning; Cade's boastings added liveliness to the second part of *Henry VI*, and the players with their rustic talk in *Love's Labour's Lost* and the *Dream* must have awakened amusing memories of many such a performance in the country. And how far the early lyric play of *Romeo and Juliet* is removed from the languid realm of romance by setting the romantic down in the midst of the familiar! Take away from the operatic hero and heroine the characters of flesh and blood which surround them, how unsubstantial would the joy and sorrow of this great tragedy appear! The greater abundance and the richer vitality of Shakespeare's living characters mark his growth as a playwright. In his earlier plays it is, as I have said, the subsidiary characters which are real, characters which are for the most part of his own invention, and not to be found in the old plays or romances from which he took his stories—they represent the encroachments of real people and daily life upon his romantic or melodramatic plots. And more and more the real people increase in vividness and numbers and begin to push the stage-characters aside. In Shakespeare's early masterpiece, the *Dream*, the principal parts are still performed by stock figures; the puzzled lovers are indistinguishable from each other, and 'merely' as they have been described, 'the abstract "Hes" and "Shes" of the conventional love-story,' while Snug and Snout and Quince and Bottom are in the background; but in *The Merchant of Venice*, written a little later, the characters who play the principal parts in this fantastic drama, Antonio, Shylock, Portia, have become so human and so living, and we are so convinced that they are real, that we accept everything else as a matter of course: we never stop to remark how absurd are the things they do. Equally absurd are the stories of the three great central comedies; but we think only of Beatrice and Benedick, of Dogberry and Verges, of Jaques, Rosalind, of Touchstone and Audrey, of Viola, Sir Toby Belch, Sir Andrew Aguecheek, of Maria, Malvolio and Feste. And when the period of great tragedy begins, the protagonists and most important characters, Brutus, Hamlet, Lear, Macbeth, Antony and Cleopatra, are the most alive, and engross the action; the stock figures fade away, and are hardly noticed.

The increase of Shakespeare's creative power shows itself, not only in the greater number of living people he puts upon the stage, and the greater importance of the parts they play, but also in the greater depth and complexity of their characters. Amid his disreputables we see the faces of those candid and fearless maidens,

Portia, Beatrice, and Rosalind; Falstaff is as subtle as any of his later creations; and certain figures, like Shylock and Malvolio, assume almost tragic proportions, and foreshadowing the tormented souls of the later tragedies, put the gay music of these comedies a little out of tune. In the plays, too, of this period we catch, in Richard II and Jaques, glimpses of that brooding and melancholy cast of temperament of which later Hamlet will prove the full expression. Here also Shakespeare achieved, what no one else has ever achieved, the creation of characters endowed with genius—for Falstaff is a genius, and Mercutio and Beatrice are not without an element of the same endowment, which will flash out later on, in Hamlet and Cleopatra. Another and unique manifestation of Shakespeare's power now makes its appearance, the portrayal of the growth or decay of human character. We note it first in the change produced in Beatrice and Benedick, when their realization of Hero's tragedy melts all that is hard and frozen in their natures; as it is afterwards made more profoundly manifest in the change in Macbeth and in Lady Macbeth after Duncan's murder, in Othello after his mind is poisoned by Iago, and, above all, in the magnificent redemption of Lear—the contrast between his brutal arrogance at first, and, when he awakes from his madness, his divine humility of soul.

There is yet another aspect of Shakespeare's power in which, among all character creators who followed in his footsteps, he stands alone. The people in the works

of other playwrights or novelists, however living, are
yet perspicuous beings; we see their motives and understand them in a way we seldom or never understand
people in real life. Real people will now and then surprise, and even astonish us with what they say and do:
we can never quite predict their future actions; but this
element of inexplicability, which at the same time in-
vites and eludes analysis, Shakespeare has given to characters like Falstaff, and Hamlet, and Cleopatra. As Dr.
Bradley finely says, 'they are inexhaustible. You feel
that, if they were alive and you spent your whole life
with them . . . they would continue every day to surprise, perplex, and delight you.' And they remain for
us like certain personages in history, like Mary Queen
of Scots, like Queen Elizabeth, like Napoleon, the subject of infinite discussion. Our sense of their reality is
heightened and quickened by our inability to see
through them and find any formula to explain them.[3]
Of all of these characters the most baffling is Hamlet;
and the fact that we cannot explain him, that he seems
unable to explain himself, is perhaps what makes this
imaginary being seem in a way more real than any real
person who ever lived.

If Shakespeare had died when he had written *Hamlet*, we might have thought that he had reached, at the
age of thirty-seven, a point, not only as a poet, but as
a dramatist, beyond which he could go no further. But

[3] *Les caractères qu'on saisit entièrement, qu'on analyse avec certi-
tude sont déjà morts.* Maeterlinck, *Macbeth*, p. xix.

in the great Michelangelesque figures which follow, in *Othello*, *Lear*, *Macbeth*, and *Coriolanus*, he brings to life beings of such colossal power, that when we turn back to his earlier plays, and gaze at the distance we have travelled, we almost grow giddy and are terrified by our vertiginous advance.

There is yet another way in which Shakespeare leapt beyond what might have seemed the limits of possible achievement. De Quincey maintained that Shakespeare, with his exquisite feeling for femininity, was the creator of the beauty of character in women; a beauty which had never been seen before, even in a dream, until he called into radiant life those radiant beings, Portia, Beatrice, Perdita, Desdemona, Imogen, Hermione, and so many others. This is a violent over-statement; we have only to think of Nausicaa and Helen and the Beatrice of the *Vita Nuova* to disprove it; but Shakespeare certainly did create in his living though non-human beings, what is a new world of creatures. There were, Lamb said, no fairies in our literature before Shakespeare, and not only did he invent that race of airy creatures who dance and sing in the *Dream*, but at the end of his career he performs, in the full maturity of his powers, an even more amazing miracle, and brings to life those most strange and wonderful beings, Ariel and Caliban, who are not human, but who arrest and affect us as if they were.

If we compare the Puck of the earlier period with the Ariel of *The Tempest*, the difference between the two cannot escape our notice. Puck is nothing more than a type of fairy; while the affectionate, petulant Ariel, swift and bright as lightning, is an individual, and yet a non-human creature. Caliban is another being of this kind, who is endowed with all the reality of a living person.

I have attempted elsewhere [4] to show the important part which Caliban plays in the history of esthetic criticism. Art was for long held to be the 'imitation of nature,' the description of what existed, or of what people believed to exist; but when Dryden, the convinced exponent of this neo-classical theory, came to account for Caliban, he said that in Caliban, 'a person which was not in Nature,' but who possessed a character of his own, and a 'language as hobgoblin as his person,' Shakespeare had allowed himself 'a boldness which at first sight would appear intolerable.' And yet Shakespeare had created him; and from this admission, and from the word 'create,' which Dryden borrowed from theology to describe such boldness, we can date the dawning perception of the artist's 'creative' gift, his godlike power, unrecognized by the ancients, to bring to life imagined people, and fashion new, authentic, and yet non-existing worlds. Nine-tenths of criticism consists in the repetition of what has been said by former critics, and for more than a hundred years it was with special reference to Caliban that Shakespeare's gift of creation was discussed.

[4] *Words and Idioms*, pp. 91-93.

We have grown tired of the words 'create,' 'creative,' so indiscriminately are they used; but a more precise knowledge of how they entered the language, and the need, with reference to Shakespeare, for which they were adopted, may help to restore a sharper edge and more precise meaning to these blunted, but indispensable, tools of thought.

II

This presentation of living, complex, self-subsistent beings was not, of course, an absolutely new invention of Shakespeare's. And yet when we think of the literature before his time, how few of the characters there depicted seem to possess an independent existence of their own. The Achilles and the Agamemnon of Homer are endowed with the gift of life; Nausicaa is clad in an exquisite immortality, and Ulysses fills the *Odyssey* with his own vitality. But in my memory of the Greek drama I find ideal types and noble figures, but few or no characters which exist apart from the plays in which they appear, and from whose plots their actions and their characters are deduced.[5]

This self-subsistence, this independence of the work

[5] 'Character-creation,' in the sense in which we use the phrase, has never been an element of great importance in classical and Continental literature. Continental writers, whose ideal has been the classical one of turning events into ideas, and making them food for thought, have found typical figures, rather than 'characters,' more transparent vehicles for their study of human passions and relations. The personages of Corneille, Racine, and Molière are

in which they play their parts, is what makes the difference between a type and what we call a 'character.' The characters are more complex, more surprising; they are made of a different and more vital substance; no sooner are they brought into existence than they seem to have existed always; and often they seem to be thinking of something else than what ought to concern them in the scenes in which they appear. And when the curtain falls, or the novel ends, they go on living in our imaginations and remain as real to us as our familiar friends.

Although we may find earlier traces of this Promethean power of creating human beings, and note in Chaucer its earliest appearance in our literature, yet its development in Shakespeare is so amazing and incredible that it seems like a great innovation, as something original and almost unknown before.

'In this part of his performance,' as Dr. Johnson said, 'he had none to imitate, but has himself been imitated by all succeeding writers.' He created a world of his own, and filled it with inhabitants of his own creation: with such a variety, indeed, and multitude of living beings that he has been reproached with making the real world seem almost empty in comparison. Although

---

more types than unique individuals, like the great figures of French fiction. There are exceptions of course; Shakespeare's contemporary, Cervantes, created living beings in Don Quixote and Sancho Panza; there are the Russian novelists, and there is Proust. But the Russians and Proust at least have been much influenced by the English novelists, and may be counted among Shakespeare's offspring.

this power is commonly regarded as Shakespeare's
greatest gift, no one of our critics, as far as I know,
with but one exception, has attempted to make a clear
distinction between the typical figures of ordinary plays
and the living and complex characters of the Shakespearean drama. The exception is that obscure and almost forgotten diplomatist and official of the eighteenth
century, Maurice Morgann, who published anonymously, in 1777, one small masterpiece of criticism, an
Essay on the Dramatic Character of Sir John Falstaff,[6]
in which he deals with this question in a profoundly
interesting way. What is the essential difference, he
asks, between Shakespeare's characters and the characters of other playwrights? The answer he gives—and I
think it is essentially a true one—can be paraphrased as
follows. No personage can be put whole into a work of
art: the writer only presents the qualities and aspects
which he needs for his purpose. In other playwrights,
the parts which are not seen do not, in fact, exist in
their makers' imagination: they have told us all they
know about them, there is nothing more in these figures,
as they conceive them, than what we see; and their in-

[6] For a fuller account of this essay, see Dr. Bradley's *Oxford
Lectures on Poetry*, pp. 274-275. The essay is reprinted in Mr. Nicol
Smith's *Eighteenth Century Essays on Shakespeare*, and, edited by
W. A. Gill, is published by the Oxford Press in a separate volume.
Morgann is said to have ordered all the other writing to be burned
at his death.

Professor Stoll prints in his *Shakespeare Studies* a long and learned
essay contradicting and attempting to refute Morgann point by
point.

teriors are, as we may put it, filled, like dolls, with sawdust.

But Shakespeare's characters, or at least the living ones among them (for many of his personages are merely types), are conceived with such an intensity of imagination that they become living and independent organisms, in which each part depends upon, and implies, the complete person. Although we see them in part only, yet from these glimpses we unconsciously infer the parts we do not see; and when Shakespeare makes them speak or act, as he sometimes does, out of these inferred, but unportrayed, aspects of their nature he produces an astonishing effect of unforeseen, yet inevitable, reality and truth.

III

Among the benefits which critics bestow upon us, the greatest one is their classifications, the distinctions which they establish between different kinds of artistic powers and achievements, and the ways those powers and achievements affect us. Of these familiar examples are the discrimination made by Shaftesbury between the sensual, and the esthetic, appeal of beauty; Lessing's delineation of the respective domains of poetry and the plastic arts, the distinction made by German critics between Genius and Talent, and the more vague, and yet indispensable contrast, first analyzed by Goethe and Schiller, between Classical and Romantic art. To these may be added the distinction, becoming now clearer and clearer, between Creation and Invention. Those differentiations and classifications, like those of the botanists and zoologists, seem so obvious when they are pointed out, and the words which express them are so familiar to us, that we are hardly aware of the niceness of observation, the effort of thought which were needed to establish and to name them; and often we forget who it was who first forged for our thinking these familiar tools of thought.

The distinction, first pointed out by Morgann, between the typical or, as we should call them, the 'two-dimensional' characters of the ordinary drama, and the figures 'in the round' which Shakespeare creates, is one, to my mind, of capital importance, but one upon which our English critics, as I have said, have hardly laid sufficient emphasis.[7] We can find examples of it in the art of painting, as well as in that of literature, for there are great portraits like Titian's *Homme au Gant*, for instance, his *Paul III* at Naples, or some of Raphael's portraits, which possess this Shakespearean quality of independent existence, and look at us from

[7] Hazlitt is the only other writer I know of who has emphasized this distinction. Shakespeare, he says, 'does not present us with groups of stage-puppets or poetical machines making set speeches on human life, and acting from a calculation of ostensible motives, but he brings living men and women on the scene, who speak and act from real feelings, according to the ebbs and flows of passion, without the least tincture of the pedantry of logic or rhetoric.' (*Characters of Shakespeare's Plays*, 1817, p. 96). Elsewhere Hazlitt says that Shakespeare 'produced a world of men and women as distinct, as true and as various as those that exist in nature' (*Ibid.*, p. 218).

their canvases like people whom we cannot think of as being dead. Perhaps of all painters it was Rembrandt who most often made his portraits into deep and real and complex beings, who live and breathe in their own right. But it is in literature, and especially in Shakespeare, that this distinction is most apparent, and, as an illustration of it, I will quote from the acute German critic, Levin Schücking, the contrast he draws between the shadowy character of Miranda in *The Tempest* and the living figure of Perdita in the *Winter's Tale*.

'Perdita also is a child of nature, a king's daughter who has grown up among simple shepherd folk. . . . But she is endowed with the whole wealth of personal touches which go to make up Shakespearean character. She is modest, unassuming, not submissive, however, but independent, full of natural dignity, frank, gay, adroit, sparkling with youthful vivacity, intelligent with all sorts of carefully cultivated little interests, . . . profoundly sincere, full of genuine feeling and tender reverence, confident and brave. What an exuberant and intense vitality! Compared with her, Miranda appears like a silhouette held beside a fully coloured oil-painting. How very few qualities can be predicated of her!'

Hotspur is not a very complex character, yet another foreign critic, after describing the racy details of his speech after his victory of Holmedon, says:

'With such solicitude, with such minute attention to tricks, flaws, whims, humours, and habits, all deduced from his temperament, from the rapid flow of his blood, from his build of body, and from his life on horseback and in the field, has Shakespeare executed this heroic character. Restless gait, stammering speech, forgetfulness, absence of mind, he overlooks nothing as being too trivial. Hotspur portrays himself in every phrase he utters, without ever saying a word directly about himself, and behind his outward, superficial peculiarities, we see into the deeper and more significant characteristics from which they spring. These, too, are closely interwoven; these, too, reveal themselves in his lightest words. We hear the same hero whom pride, sense of honour, spirit of independence, and intrepidity inspire with the sublimest utterances, at other times chatting, jesting, and even talking nonsense. The jests and nonsense are an integral part of the real human being; in them, too, one side of his real nature reveals itself. . . . In classical tragedy, French, German, or Danish, the hero is too solemn to talk nonsense and too lifeless to jest.' [8]

Hotspur, our analyst adds, has the defects of his qualities: he is contentious, jealous in his ambition, and cannot bear to hear anyone else praised: he judges hastily, according to appearances, and, of course, lacks any esthetic feeling. A proud, self-reliant, unscrupulous rebel, caring neither for State, King, nor Commons, he is a hero of the feudal ages—'a marvellous figure as Shakespeare has projected him, stammering, absent, turbulent, witty, now simple, now magniloquent. His

[8] Brandes, p. 190.

hauberk clatters on his breast, his spurs jingle at his heel, wit flashes from his lips, while he moves and has his being in a nimbus of renown.'

IV

It is beyond the competence of the critic to explain such creative power; he approaches there the ultimate secret of existence, the mystery by means of which this many-peopled world has been brought into being. But just as the critic, like the botanist or zoologist, can note and describe and classify the products of this creative process, and even sometimes spy upon the great Creator at his work, so we may note the occasions which called forth Shakespeare's powers, observe the subtle touches, the lights and shades and delicate half-tints, the interplay and fusion of idiosyncrasies and qualities, by means of which he presents his people as real as life before us.

As he worked over an old play, or dramatized some old story, it is plain that some shadowy figure would arouse Shakespeare's interest and seize upon his imagination; he would perceive in it the suggestion of something human, something pathetic or absurd; and then, like the God of Michelangelo's fresco, he would touch it with his finger and endow it with the gift of life. Sometimes these figures will spring to life at once and express the very essence of themselves in the first words they utter: 'By my troth, Nerissa, my little body is aweary of this great world.'—'Three thousand ducats; well?'—Portia and Shylock stand before us as they speak. 'Now, Hal, what time of the day is it, lad?' 'Keep up your bright swords, for the dew will rust them'—these phrases present Falstaff and Othello at once before our eyes. And when Cleopatra, in her first words, says to Antony,

If it be love indeed, tell me how much,

does not the slow languor of this line put us under the spell at once of Antony's 'serpent of old Nile'? Other characters seem to hang on his hands at first, and only say what they have to say in conventional phrases. But as his play progresses Shakespeare begins to form a deeper conception of their natures, as for instance of 'the serpent of old Nile,' who changes her character as the play progresses, until at last she meets her death with a splendour of heroism which is quite incompatible with her earlier portrayal. Shakespeare does not revise his earlier descriptions, but leaves them unchanged, so that we can watch the process of growth as it took place in his own mind as he proceeded. This happens with Ariel; indeed in the scene in which Ariel makes his earliest appearance, we seem to catch Shakespeare's godlike genius in the very act of creation. Ariel comes on the scene a figure lightly and carelessly formed, a mere useful fairy, who reluctantly renders various services, and must be held in check and treated with severity.

He speaks at first with the dull bombast which Shakespeare is apt to put into the mouths of his dramatic
mechanisms; and Prospero calls him 'sullen,' 'malig-
nant,' 'dull.' But the poor enslaved spirit begs for liberty, and at that petition the miracle happens, a beautiful creature springs to life in Shakespeare's mind—the
most delicate creation, as Sir Walter Scott described
him, of Shakespeare's imagination. He endows at that
moment this airy creature, 'thou who art but air,' with
immortal life, and promises him his freedom if he will
carry out certain requests. When, after performing the
first of these, Ariel returns in a few moments, Prospero
calls him 'my quaint Ariel'; and when he comes back
after another few minutes from a second errand, he is
endowed with the aerial gift of music, and the enchanted
Ferdinand follows him as he sings two of the most
magical and unearthly songs in our literature. Prospero
now addresses him as 'delicate Ariel,' 'spirit, fine spirit,'
and renews the promise to set him free; 'Thou shalt be
as free as mountain winds,' he says in a phrase finely
suggesting that liberation from human cares, from the
life of humanity itself, which Ariel longs for. After
this Ariel is to Prospero a loved creature, 'my tricksy
spirit' he addresses him, 'my delicate Ariel,' 'my bird';
and when Ariel at the prospect of his liberation, puts
into song the passionless joy of nature he longs for,

> *Merrily, merrily shall I live now*
> *Under the blossom that hangs on the bough,*

'Why, that's my dainty Ariel! I shall miss thee,' Prospero says; and in his last speech dismisses him sadly: 'My Ariel, chick . . . to the elements be free, and fare thou well!'; and thus Ariel vanishes from the world of men to live for ever in their imaginations.[9]

v

As in reading Shakespeare's plays we note this development of his power of endowing with life the figures he portrays, we note also, as its consequences, the gradual shift from the drama of circumstance to a new kind of drama, that of character. From the theatrical comedies of mistaken identity he passes to comedies of self-delusion; from tragedies of circumstances to tragedies produced by the clash of characters in their conflicts with each other—Othello with Iago, for instance, and Troilus with Cressida, and Antony with Cleopatra. And with these he creates also tragedies due to the struggle of a great hero with himself. Romeo, Richard II, and Richard III contend with outward forces, but very little with themselves; their natures are not divided; but in the later tragedies we find play after play in which the combatant powers within the hero's soul are dramatized: we see Brutus 'with himself at war,' Hamlet conscious of the contending forces within him, and Lear, Macbeth, and Coriolanus involved in gigantic struggles

[9] I am indebted for the above analysis to A. C. Benson's fine study of Ariel, in *A Book of Homage to Shakespeare*, p. 197.

with their own natures, which can only end in insanity or death. Such dramas of the clash of character, such psychological tragedies of inner conflict, Shakespeare fits as best he can into the plots and old stories which he finds at hand. These crazy old structures he rebuilds bit by bit in shining marble, leaving, however, portions of the original edifice standing as they were.

Froude once described oratory as the harlot of the arts; and it often seems as if Shakespeare regarded drama as equally deserving of this appellation. With what contempt he treats his plots; any hackneyed theatrical device or stage trick he considers good enough for his audience, he repeats them over and over again without scruple; and the plays of the last period are so absurd in plots and action that he seems to be flouting his audience with a kind of cynical contempt. 'To remark upon the folly of the fiction,' as Dr. Johnson says of *Cymbeline*, 'the absurdity of the conduct . . . and the impossibility of the events in any system of life, were to waste criticism upon unresisting imbecility, upon faults too evident for detection, and too gross for aggravation.'

The carelessness of what Keats called 'Shakespeare's indolent and kingly gaze' shows itself, not only in his treatment of plots and action, but also in the inconsistencies of his characters with the dramas in which they play their parts. A great deal of criticism has been directed of late to these inconsistencies, which, when our attention has been called to them, are glaring enough. These violations of character are often due to the necessities of the play, the need to force back into the crude framework of old plots characters which, at Shakespeare's vitalizing touch, have so outgrown the situations in which they figure that we are shocked, and properly shocked, at the dissonance between what they are and what they do—as, for instance, when the saintly Isabella, in *Measure for Measure*, connives without reluctance in the ugly trick by which the Duke (who also acts completely out of character) traps Angelo into marriage, and then most incongruously pairs off with him in the final scene.

Often Shakespeare endows his personages with too great a vitality for the play in which they figure, and Dryden records the tradition that Shakespeare himself said that he was forced to kill Mercutio in the third act of *Romeo and Juliet* to prevent Mercutio from killing him. It has already been noted how Shylock and Malvolio grow to a tragic height which somewhat overshadows the gay comedies in which they make their appearance. In Lear Shakespeare created a character which ran away with him more completely perhaps than any other, and makes still more absurd and fantastic the absurd and fantastic plot of that tragedy.[10] But Shakespeare could seldom refuse to give his chance to any character that came to life on his hands; often he

[10] Tolstoy's plain recital of the story of King Lear is the most effective and amusing feature of that anti-Shakespeare Manifesto in which the great old novelist proves himself to be about as mad as the great old King.

will let the action stand still while he interpolates incidents invented only for the purpose of displaying its
idiosyncrasies; and, perhaps, like Cervantes with Don
Quixote, like Sterne with Uncle Toby, or Dickens with
Mr. Pickwick, he could not help it. Sir Walter Scott
was, at however great a distance, more like Shakespeare
than any other writer, and those who have written best
about Shakespeare's character, Bagehot and Leslie
Stephen and Dr. Bradley, have all laid emphasis upon
this likeness. Scott, like Shakespeare, had no artistic
conscience; he cared little for fame, and much for the
goods of this world, for money and social position, and
tried to achieve these by providing harmless amuse-
ment for the public. But he was, like Shakespeare, a
great artist and character-creator, and with his large and
tolerant acceptance of human nature, his sympathy with
the enjoyments, the passions and ambitions of all sorts
of people, he could enter into the inner self of many
kinds of men. Like Shakespeare, too, he was bothered
by characters who would burst through the trammels
of his plots and insist on acting and speaking for themselves. Scott complained of this himself,[11] and more

[11] In a curious and most self-revealing document (which his
biographers and critics seem to have neglected), Scott's Introduction
to the *Fortunes of Nigel*, he gives an account of his interview with
his own genius, whom he found, after long search, in a dark and
vaulted room at the back of Constable's shop in Edinburgh, and
where this 'Eidolon,' this 'Vision of the Author of Waverley,' says:
'I think there is a demon who seats himself on the feather of my
pen when I begin to write, and leads it astray from the purpose. . . .
When I light on such a character as Bailie Jarvie, or Dalgetty, my

than once remarked on the way in which—in spite of his most obstinate determination to the contrary—the greatest rogue on his canvas would stand out as the most conspicuous figure.

An odd instance of how a character can come to life and take possession of the work in which he is intended to play only a minor part is Scott's *Legend of Montrose,* a novel which Scott meant to be a romance of tragedy and fate and romantic warfare in the Highlands. But when, almost at the beginning, the common-sense, boring figure of Dugald Dalgetty steps into the story, he takes command at once, and at the sound of his prosaic voice the romantic figures with their tale of mystery seem to vanish like ghosts.

But Shakespeare's carelessness shows itself, not only in the inconstancy of his characters with the plots in which they figure—there are inconsistencies, and plenty of them, to be observed in the characters themselves. Thus, for instance, his villains, like Iago and Edmund, confess their villainy with the utmost frankness, and (what no villains would ever do) they pay the most

---

imagination brightens, and my conception becomes clearer at every step which I make in his company, although it leads me many a weary mile away from the regular road, and forces me to leap hedge and ditch to get back into the route again. If I resist the temptation, as you advise me, my thoughts become prosy, flat, and dull; I write painfully to myself, and under a consciousness of flagging which makes me flag still more; the sunshine with which fancy had invested the incidents, departs from them, and leaves everything dull and gloomy. . . . In short, sir, on such occasions, I think I am bewitched.'

generous tributes to the noble qualities of their victims. His virtuous characters are equally frank about their own virtues, boasting of them, like Cordelia, with a complacency that is completely out of character. Out of character, too, are the fine phrases which he puts into prosaic mouths, the profound wisdom of the advice given by the shallow-pated Polonius to Laertes, or the prosaic Queen's poetic description of Ophelia's death. Our romantic critics have woven tangles of elaborate theory to justify these inconsistencies; but more recent commentators have shown that they are trying to explain what stands in need of no explanation. For, as they point out, Shakespeare's art-form retained many of the primitive elements of archaic drama; and to fix clearly in the minds of the audience the parts his personages were meant to play, he made them define at once their virtues or their vices in speeches which are not pieces of psychological realism, but resemble those scrolls which in primitive pictures proceed out of the mouths of the figures and proclaim 'I am,' etc.

Moreover, as the same critics point out, the great set speeches of the plays are also very often out of character. An Elizabethan drama was, as Coleridge perceived in one of the flashes of his dark lantern, 'something between a recitation and a re-presentation'; it was built, as a later critic has put it, 'upon the vigour and beauty of speech. We may suppose that at its best the mere speaking of the plays was a very brilliant thing, comparable to *bel canto*, or a pianist's virtuosity.'

We do it wrong, being so majestical,
To offer it the show of violence;
For it is, as the air, invulnerable,
And our vain blows malicious mockery.

Death, that hath suck'd the honey of thy breath,
Hath had no power yet upon thy beauty:
Thou art not conquer'd; beauty's ensign yet
Is crimson in thy lips and in thy cheeks,
And death's pale flag is not advanced there.

Speeches like these were recited to audiences who loved fine language as we love music, and who by no means cared, as we care, for consistency of character. Plangent declamation, or passages made splendid by this overplus of diction, this fine-broken starlight of fine words, was what they liked; and this led to what has been called 'episodic intensification' on Shakespeare's part, so that his plays are not so much organic wholes as a series of momentarily effective episodes, episodes in which he 'makes his character say what is effective, right, and appropriate to the occasion, without troubling overmuch to reflect whether the words may not possibly conflict with some other passage.'

These words are Goethe's, and their application in detail to the plays has been carried out in recent years by German critics, the results of whose investigations are more or less summed up in the book of Schücking I have mentioned. How much has Shakespeare's fame as a portrayer of character been damaged by this criticism? It has, I think, been damaged; even his greatest creations hardly seem the miracles and marvels that once we thought them; and many inconsistencies so many of which English critics have explained as deep subtleties of insight, are now seen to be real inconsistencies that Shakespeare knew would pass unnoticed in the stage-performance, which was all he cared for, since he did not write his plays to be read and studied by future generations. And yet, for the real comprehension of Shakespeare's characters it is best not to see them looming through a cloud of incense, but fashioned as he fashioned them for their appearance on the stage.

VI

The story is well known of the eighteenth-century French sculptor in Rome, who, after praising a horse modelled by himself, and pointing out how faulty in comparison was the horse of Marcus Aurelius on the Capitol, paused for a moment, sighed, took a pinch of snuff, and then said: 'All the same, gentlemen, it must be admitted that that wretched horse up there is alive; —and this one of mine is dead.'

Since Shakespeare's characters, with all their faults in modelling, are still so living that no violations can really do them violence, the temptation to try to peer a little more closely into his workshop is hard to resist. Such an attempt may not be perhaps without some practical advantage as well. People are still writing novels,

and it is from Shakespeare that our great English novelists have learned their art of creating characters and
projecting them in action. It has been pointed out that
the three plays in which Prince Hal figures may be described as the first of the many-centred, miscellaneous
English novels which are held together by character
rather than by plot; and, indeed, as character-creation
is regarded as the very essence of English fiction, the
sine qua non of novel writing, any examination of the
most amazing manifestation of this power will not be
without a modern interest.

That Shakespeare drew the names and actions of most
of his personages from books is known to everybody;
and an examination of how he used his sources, and
especially Plutarch's *Lives*, shows how he seized upon
many of their idiosyncrasies and characteristic utterances
to give them the quality of life. How far he made use
of living models we have, of course, little or no evidence save that of Aubrey, who preserved the tradition
that the character of Dogberry was studied from a live
original—from a constable at Grendon, in Buckingham-
shire, through which village Shakespeare often passed.

On *a priori* grounds it seems safe to say that Shakespeare's characters were the result of observation, for
they possess that convincing quality of figures drawn
from the life. Most revealing to my mind is a remark
of Falstaff's, who, after a subtle analysis of Shallow's
character, goes on to say: 'I will devise matter enough
out of this Shallow to keep Prince Henry in continual

laughter for the wearing out of six fashions.' We cannot but feel that Shakespeare's disreputables, his bawds, and pimps, and boasters, his nincompoops and fools and dullards, his complacent old shallow-pates, were drawn from living models, and were the 'mellow fruit,' as Sir Edmund Chambers has described them, 'of that deliberate realistic observation of the Anglo-Saxon idiosyncrasies of speech and thought, as they revealed themselves to him in burgess and rustic, which links Shakespeare to Chaucer, and of all his innumerable gifts is perhaps his most inalienable birthright'; [12] and that from these models he could create, like Shelley's poet, 'forms more real than living man'; that, in fact, those 'nurslings of immortality,' his rout of outrageous scoundrels, must have once possessed their pale counterparts on earth.

His vigilance of observation must, we feel, have been, as Dr. Johnson says, 'in the highest degree curious and attentive'; almost all original and native excellence, Dr. Johnson adds, 'proceeds from vigilance of observation'; and the works of the great novelists who followed after and imitated Shakespeare prove that they, too, possessed this vigilance of observation, which, indeed, often got them into trouble by their inveterate habit of putting real people into their books.[13]

[12] *Shakespeare: A Survey*, p. 132.
[13] Novelists whose aim is to create character are, and must be, cannibals. They must have models, they must live on the living; and often, like Tolstoy and Scott and Dickens, they may be counted as members of those tribes who cook and eat their own parents. But

It has been pointed out by an eminent critic that original characters taken at first hand from nature must not only be seen to be known, but must be liked to be living. Shakespeare's evident love for his characters, and especially the most disreputable of them, his delight that they should be exactly what they are—gives a warmth to the portrayal of their existence which helps them to exist in our imaginations also.[14] This habit of falling in love with his characters is one of the things which give Shakespeare his power of identifying himself with them, of placing himself, as it were, in their

---

the debt we all owe to them is so beyond computation, that the victims of their laudable voracity should not complain too much. There is, however, a more serious indictment which might be drawn up against the English novel, held together, as far as it is held together at all, by character, rather than by plot. Taking a general view of our novels from the classical and Continental standpoint suggested in a former note, must we not regard them, in spite of—and even perhaps on account of—their swarming abundance of living characters, somewhat trivial and superficial as analyses of life? Are not most of these big books rather like big picnics, or expeditions, or religious or political outings, at which a lot of odd people indulge in irrelevant horse-play, or listen to harangues and sermons, and then pair off for no especial reason? Do not the separate episodes in them count more than the general impression they create? Have the individuals more than a casual relation to the book in which they happen to appear? Could not almost any of the characters—Mrs. Gamp, or Pecksniff, or Mr. Micawber—in one of Dickens's novels have figured just as well in any of the others? And hasn't this habit of creating living beings embarrassed even the most consummate of our artists, when he endangered the moral scheme of his moral epic by making his Devil so much more alive and interesting than his God?

[14] The wealth of Shakespeare's creative genius is shown, Sir Walter Raleigh says, in his superfluous creations, in the way that a

skins and participating in all their thoughts and feelings. Here I may avail myself of another gleam from Coleridge's criticism. 'It is easy,' he says, 'to clothe imaginary beings with our own thoughts and feelings; but to send ourselves out of ourselves, to *think* ourselves into the thoughts and feelings of beings in circumstances wholly and strangely different from our own, *hic labor, hoc opus;* and who has achieved it? perhaps only Shakespeare.' Shakespeare not only leaps into the skins of the most unlikely characters, but he makes us take the same leap with him: suddenly, without warning, we find ourselves thinking the thoughts of the most improper kinds of people; we see life as some old whore, like Mrs. Overdone, or Mrs. Quickly, or a pimp like Pompey, see it; or, becoming as infamous as the infamous Parolles, we say to ourselves with him, 'Simply the thing I am shall make me live.'

How much of himself Shakespeare put into his creations, to what extent he cut himself in pieces, and put one of his moods or his experiences into one character and another in another, has been the subject of much

---

figure which is a mere mechanism in the plot may suddenly come to life, and so endear himself to his maker, that he cannot be allowed to perform the distasteful duty for which he was created. Barnardine, in *Measure for Measure*, the self-confessed murderer, is an instance of this. He was to be executed in order that his head should be substituted for that of Claudio, but when summoned from his cell for that purpose he absolutely refuses: 'I will not consent to die this day, that's certain.' 'Not a word,' he says to the Duke, who realizes that his execution is impossible, and is forced to pardon him in the end.

discussion; and here again we may avail ourselves of Coleridge's lantern, who suggests that his method was to conceive of some intellectual or moral faculty of his own as carried to a morbid excess, and then to place himself, thus mutilated and diseased, in the circumstances which make the excess apparent in comic or tragic relief.

VII

But Shakespeare's ways of performing his miracles of character-creation must remain, as with all other miracles, inscrutable to us in the end. Of that mysterious process of the human mind, called the creative faculty, we know almost nothing: we are able, however, to observe more clearly the means by which he presents the men and women he creates before our eyes. He shows them in action, of course, and brings one character into sharp relief by its contrast with another, Richard II with Bolingbroke, the fiery Antony with the cold Octavius, Cordelia with her awful sisters, and the contrast which Hamlet himself draws between his paralysis of thought and the spirit of that delicate and tender Prince, young Fortinbras, eager and rash to face 'all that fortune, death and danger dare, even for an eggshell.' Still more subtly, Shakespeare lets us see his characters mirrored in the eyes of others: Lady Macbeth's fear of Macbeth's nature, and Cæsar's mistrust of Cassius—'He thinks too much: such men are dangerous,' and that of Brutus for Cicero, in his profound remark that Cicero 'will never follow any thing that other men begin'? What could be more vivid than Falstaff's portrait of Justice Shallow, or the description Ulysses gives of the wanton Cressida,

> *There's language in her eye, her cheek, her lip,*
> *Nay, her foot speaks.*

The effect of these revelations is sometimes appalling; sometimes a face seen thus in the horror of another's eyes takes on an awful aspect, as when for instance, in Shakespeare's early tragedy, Juliet's good-natured old nurse advises Juliet to forget her banished lover and marry Paris—to whom she says Romeo is but a dishclout in comparison, and, at the sight of treachery in that leering face—the first appearance, it has been described, of that spiritual evil which blackens and makes so terrible the later tragedies—Juliet cries out, 'Ancient damnation!' in sudden horror, 'O most wicked fiend!'

In scenes of comedy this method of showing people reflected in each other's eyes is often used to enhance the comic effect; and when, as sometimes happens, Shakespeare's people caricature each other, with what vigorous strokes these caricatures are drawn! Hotspur's description of 'the nimble-footed, madcap Prince of Wales' finds a more than adequate reply in what the Prince says of Hotspur, 'he that kills me some six or seven dozen of Scots at a breakfast, washes his hands, and says to his wife, "Fie upon this quiet life! I want work." "O my sweet Harry," says she, "how many hast thou killed today?" "Give my roan horse a drench," says he, and answers, "some fourteen," an hour after, "a trifle, a trifle." '

Of all the reflections and flashings of faces in the eyes of others, perhaps the most marvellous are found in that magnificent palace of mirrors and reflecting glasses, *Antony and Cleopatra*—Cleopatra, as Enobarbus saw her, seated in her barge that was like a burnished throne; his description of her infinite variety, which age could not wither, and Cleopatra's portrait of Antony,

> *For his bounty,*
> *There was no winter in't, an autumn 'twas*
> *That grew the more by reaping; his delights*
> *Were dolphin-like, they show'd his back above*
> *The element they liv'd in—*

and then this same 'Emperor Antony,' seen simply as an 'old ruffian' in the steely eyes of Octavius. In general we may say that what Shakespeare's characters are is not told to the reader—he must infer their natures from no one description, but from the various impressions they make on their friends and enemies—for each person in a play of Shakespeare is a mirror in which the others are reflected—and from their own visions of themselves, the explanations they give of their own natures.

VIII

Shakespeare's characters are much given to self-portrayal; in the earlier plays these take the archaic form, as we have seen, of speeches which are often completely out of character, and merely intended to make clear to the audience the parts they are about to play—as Richard Crookback, for instance, on his first appearance tells us frankly, 'I am determined to prove a villain.' But in his later plays Shakespeare uses this method of self-portrayal on the part of his characters to present before us true, profound and astonishing revelations of their souls and circumstances—as when, for instance, Macbeth, on the news of his enemies' approach, says,

> *I have liv'd long enough; my way of life*
> *Is fall'n into the sere, the yellow leaf;*

and Antony, who, 'with half the bulk o' the world' had played as he pleased, when, knowing that he is ruined, and believing that Cleopatra has betrayed him, pauses before committing suicide to make a marvellous, long-drawn comparison between himself and the dissolving clouds of sunset (*A. and C.*, IV, xii), or when Othello in his magnificent last speech, says to the Venetian officials,

> *Speak of me as I am; . . .*
> *Of one that lov'd not wisely but too well;*
> *Of one not easily jealous, but, being wrought,*
> *Perplex'd in the extreme; of one whose hand,*

Like the base Indian, threw a pearl away
Richer than all his tribe; of one whose subdu'd eyes,
Albeit unus'd to the melting mood,
Drop tears as fast as the Arabian trees
Their medicinable gum.

In the comedies also these self-descriptions produce comic effects of the richest laughter. The fat old rogue of a Falstaff sometimes describes himself as a youth; 'What! ye knaves,' he cries to the travellers he is robbing, 'young men must live'; 'you that are old,' he gravely addresses the Lord Chief Justice, 'consider not the capacities of us that are young'; and as for his voice being broken, well, he had lost it in hollaying, and singing of anthems. And then again he pathetically admits his years; 'There live not three good men unhanged in England, and one of them is fat and grows old; God help the while! A bad world, I say.'

'I am a wise fellow; and, which is more, an officer; and, which is more, a householder; and, which is more, as pretty a piece of flesh as any in Messina; and one that knows the law, go to; and a rich fellow enough, go to; and a fellow that hath had losses; and one that hath two gowns, and everything handsome about him'; —After this self-portrait, Dogberry is surely in no need of the sexton to write him down an ass.

Shakespeare's characters will sometimes address themselves, or speak of themselves by name in the third person.

Swell'st thou, proud heart? I'll give thee scope to beat,

Richard II says in his humiliation. 'Go thy ways, old Jack; die when thou wilt,' Falstaff sighs in the scene of his exposure, and these mentions of themselves by their own names, either with Falstaff's humour, or the pathos of 'Othello's occupation's gone,' or the kind of awe with which Cæsar habitually speaks of Cæsar,

> *Danger knows full well*
> *That Cæsar is more dangerous than he—*

these self-reflections, these images of their own being in the mirrors of their own imaginations, flash for a moment in our eyes with a vividness that makes us catch our breath.

Shakespeare very often makes use of the soliloquy as a means of portraying character, making his personages think aloud, and explain, or try to explain, their motives, and describe their most secret thoughts and feelings. Our nineteenth-century dramatists regarded the soliloquy as unnatural, and in modern novels it is replaced by those dips into the stream of consciousness which are, after all, quite as conventional a device. We may also note in Shakespeare the first appearance in literature of that most self-revealing of all devices, the daydream; as for instance, Henry VI, when he sits apart from the raging battle, exclaims, in his envy of the shepherd's lot, 'Ah! what a life were this! how sweet, how lovely!' The daydream in Shakespeare is apt, as in life, to take the form of an imagined conversation in which the dreamer of the dream always comes off best. Thus, when Philip the Bastard is suddenly knighted by King John he at once begins to imagine himself entertaining a distinguished traveller in a condescending fashion.

> *And when my knightly stomach is suffic'd,*
> *Why then I suck my teeth, and catechize*
> *My picked man of countries: 'My dear sir,'—*
> *Thus, leaning on my elbow, I begin,—*
> *'I shall beseech you'—*

Thus also Malvolio, when he imagines himself Olivia's husband, how, sitting in state in his branched-velvet gown he sends, 'after a demure travel of regard,' for Sir Toby Belch, and seven of his people with an obedient start go to seek him, 'I frown the while; and perchance wind up my watch . . . Toby approaches; curtsies there to me . . . I extend my hand to him thus, quenching my familiar smile with an austere regard of control, saying, "Cousin Toby, my fortunes having cast me on your niece give me this prerogative of speech" '—But it is superfluous to transcribe this immortal scene, of which the amazing effectiveness makes one wonder why the daydream has been so neglected by most novelists except by the masters of them all, Tolstoy and Flaubert, and by the writer of the greatest novel of the world, which is all compact of daydreams, Don Quixote's daydreams of chivalrous adventure, and Sancho Panza's of his Island.

Shakespeare makes frequent use also of the dreams of sleep, but uses these mostly as parts of his plots rather than as means of character-portrayal. He finds them useful as conveying premonitions and knowledge of the future, but they are seldom as subtle and psychological as the dreams which we find—of all places! —in the Old Testament.

Another subtle device for producing the psychological illusion of reality has been noticed by Brandes—the mention, namely, of some irrelevant and often ludicrous detail, as, for instance, when Hotspur, explaining why he did not hand over the Scottish prisoners after the battle of Holmedon, describes how the courtier, perfumed like a milliner, who demanded them, informed him, among many other things, that

> *The sovereign'st thing on earth*
> *Was parmaceti for an inward bruise.*

'Why this spermaceti?' Brandes asks. 'Why this dwelling upon so trivial and ludicrous a detail? Because it is a touch of reality and begets illusion. Because we cannot see at first the reason why Percy should recall so trifling a circumstance, it seems impossible that the thing should be a mere invention. . . . If this be real, then all the rest is real, and Henry Percy stands before our eyes, covered with dust and blood, as on the field of Holmedon. We see the courtier at his side, . . .

and we hear him giving the young commander his medical advice and irritating him to the verge of frenzy.'

Prince Hal's longing for 'the poor creature small beer,' when the King, his father, was so ill, and the sight of Cleopatra hopping along the street, are other examples of Shakespeare's use of ludicrous detail—of which Lear's button is the most sublime example.

IX

But Shakespeare's main device for bringing his characters into existence is simply to make them talk themselves alive. To each living individual is given an individual way of speech: everyone possessing, in everything he says, an idiom, a diction, a rhythm, a sort of sing-song of his own, so unique and so distinctive that without reading the names of the *dramatis personæ* we can recognise each of them by his voice.

Tolstoy described this individuality of speech, this harmony of character and language, as the most important, if not the only, means of portraying character; that he found Shakespeare lacking in this gift is one of the most amazing statements in his amazing anti-Shakespeare manifesto. It is true that the stock characters in Shakespeare's plays all speak in the same way; and in *Macbeth*, for instance, the speeches of Malcolm and Donalbain, Macduff and Lennox are indistinguishable from each other—but these personages are indistinguishable in character.[15] But as soon as a living person begins to speak we shall find that all his words are his own, that his most subtle qualities are portrayed by rhythm, accent, intonation, and choice of word or image. All his idiosyncrasies seem somehow present in everything he says, as we hear all its overtones in the sound of any note in music. And more than that; each characteristic phrase, hesitation, qualification, repetition, evokes the face of the speaker before our imagination; we seem to see the raised or frowning eye-brows, the lips pursed, or pleasantly, or wryly, smiling, the teeth bared, the nostrils dilated, the head nodding, or angrily turned away. 'Sweet lord, if your lordship were at leisure,'— we see the courtier's smirk of Osric when he addresses Hamlet; the vacant face of Polonius is before us as he says to Reynaldo, 'And then, sir, does he this,—he does, —what was I about to say?' And when Beatrice tells the Prince of Arragon, 'No, sure, my lord, my mother cried; but then there was a star danced, and under that was I born'—do we not see her eyes sparkling as she makes this answer? Indeed, one of the greatest miracles of this great miracle-monger is his invention of so many individual ways of speech for such a multitude of im-

[15] It has been suggested, perhaps too subtly, that Shakespeare instinctively felt, or consciously feared, that too much individuality in the subordinate figures would diminish the bold relief in which he wished the principal characters in *Macbeth* to stand out, and so, like a good artist, modelled them in the flat: thus making us aware of his power of creating characters by its partial suppression in this play.

agined people. It is almost superfluous to give instances:
the various voices of Shakespeare's characters are familiar in our ears. The bold speech of the Bastard in
King John, the witty double-meanings of Mercutio in
Romeo and Juliet, the inimitably vulgar locutions of
the Nurse, of whom it has been said that no speech of
hers throughout the play could have been spoken by
anyone else, the chanting quality of Shylock's speech
and his use of Biblical expressions, Hotspur's thick
speech, with his words tumbling over each other from
mere impatience, Glendower's solemn style, and Caliban, with, as Dryden said, 'a speech as hobgoblin as his
person.' We may also note, with Brandes, the difference
in the speech of Beatrice and Rosalind, two of Shakespeare's wittiest heroines. Beatrice's diction is marvellous: we see, as it were, the gleam of a rapier in her
wit; the wit of Rosalind scintillates also, but with a
soft, firefly radiance that has no sting. And then Falstaff, was there ever talk that so expressed the talker
as the wonderful prose of Falstaff's speeches? Even our
Professor Stoll, after writing a long essay to destroy
the modern conception of Falstaff as a psychological
unity, falls a victim himself to the fat villain's voice. It
is his speech, not his conduct, Professor Stoll writes,
which appeals to us; 'he talks prose but is supremely
poetic, and his is in many ways the most marvellous
prose ever penned. It pulses with his vast vitality and
irrepressible spirit, it glows with the warmth of his
friendliness and good humour, it sparkles with his fancy

and wit. No prose or verse either is so heavily charged with the magnetism of a personality, or has caught so perfectly the accent and intonation of an individual human voice.' [16]

Neither in character nor in speech are Rosencrantz and Guildenstern differentiated in *Hamlet;* there are two of them only because, as Goethe said, they stand for society in general, and the social spirit could not find embodiment in an individual, but Polonius expresses himself (save in his advice to Laertes, which is quite out of character) in every word; and Hamlet's ironic phrases, his far-fetched conceits, his use of word-play and doggerel in moments of extreme excitement, make his voice the most unmistakable of all voices. Of all his tricks of speech, there is none, as Dr. Bradley has pointed out, more revealing, more intensely character-istic than this trick of verbal repetition. 'Words, words, words'—'Very like, very like'—'Thrift, thrift, Horatio' —'Except my life, except my life'; is not the very essence of his life embodied in these little phrases?

[16] *Shakespeare Studies,* p. 485. Professor Stoll, while going much further than the German critics in his thesis that Shakespeare did not create *psychologically* consistent characters, and that his per-sonages do things that are completely out of character, or rather have nothing to do with character at all, yet admits that he does give them individuality by means of the individuality of their voices and their tricks of speech. Though, but for the most part, mere 'bundles of words in verse and prose,' yet each has a 'concrete and intense reality of utterance,' an 'indefinable individuality and iden-tity of tone,' perceptible in the cast of his phrases, the sound and rhythm of his voice; and this, he describes as Shakespeare's 'greatest triumph in characterization.'

Could any number of analytic or descriptive pages have made him more alive? And the four last words he speaks, 'The rest is silence,' is the supreme expression of his being at the moment when it ceases. Even more magnificently expressive are the great last speeches of Lear and Cleopatra and Othello, when Cleopatra cries:

> *Give me my robe, put on my crown; I have*
> *Immortal longings in me—*

or when Othello, beginning:

> *Soft you; a word or two before you go—*

weaves all the colour and clang and grandeur of his life into the texture of that dying speech which no one in the world but Othello could have uttered.

x

This method which Shakespeare invented—of making his people talk themselves alive—is surely the most marvellous of all his marvellous inventions. It is from him that our great English novelists learnt the art of giving individuality to their characters by individual ways of speech. Meg Merrilies and Rob Roy both speak in Scott's novels with a vocabulary of their own; and when characters like Nicol Jarvie and Dalgetty ran away with him, he would drop everything and run after them to listen to their phrases. Of Jane Austen we may say what Pope said of Shakespeare, 'had all the speeches been printed without the very names of the persons, I believe one might have applied them with certainty to every speaker.' Dickens possessed this gift almost to madness: he created hundreds of—if not quite human—yet living beings, endowing each with a syntax, rhythm, and song, an excited or drowsy twitter of its own, a personal note, as distinctive as the note of a robin or a wren or chaffinch. Dickens overdid, no doubt, this way of letting his characters sing themselves alive; he made them reiterate their fixed ideas in tunes and cuckoo-phrases so mechanically that they became mechanisms rather than organic beings—caricatures, like, indeed, Pistol and Poins in Shakespeare, instead of characters. The successors of Dickens and his imitators have in consequence adopted methods which seem to them more profound, of description and analysis. But description, analysis, and even action, are incapable, it would seem, of creating characters with an independent existence of their own. Such characters have disappeared in consequence from our fiction, and since Dickens no novel-writer has succeeded in making any universally known figure live in our imagination. Human nature, nowadays, it has been suggested, is too complex, too self-conscious, too irresolute to be moulded into rounded characters, like those of our older writers. But does human nature change in this fashion? Are most modern women more complex than Cleopatra, or many men more self-conscious, more irresolute than Hamlet?

If, therefore, I were advising any youth of high aims, who might entertain the ambition of reviving the dead art of the English drama, or the dying art of the English novel, I should suggest to him (although he would certainly not listen) that he should study above all the speech-rhythms, the syntax, the hesitations, the tricks of phrase and verbal sing-song of the people with whom he talks; for this shimmering texture of human speech, significant as it is both with the states of soul and with the meanings and tensions and clashes of human beings in their relations with each other, is, for the writers of drama or fiction, the very stuff of life, the stuff out of which are woven plays like those of Shakespeare, novels like those of Jane Austen, Scott, and Dickens.

But, as I say, my young writer would not listen, for he belongs, and rightly belongs, to his own generation, a generation to whom the inward stream of consciousness is of more interest than conduct and individuality expressed in speech, and whose accepted prophet has declared indeed that character-creation belongs to the dead past, to a moral scheme of life which is now obsolete; and that fiction must seek its renovation by a 'diving escape' from character-creation into the 'life-flow'; into the dark stream below our conscious life of thought and reason. There, and not in the play of character, is to be found the true stuff of life; and very sad stuff it seems to me as they dredge it up. If the man of intellect dwells, so a philosopher has told us, within a dullard and holds a lunatic in leash, what praise is to be won by recording that dullard's bovine ruminations, or the monotonous ravings of that lunatic?

'But why not praise?' Reason, divine Reason answers, touching like Apollo my angry ears. 'Don't repeat the hackneyed old folly of judging things in growth by their leaves and not by their fruit; of condemning what may be a flowering plant long before it flowers. What could have seemed—what indeed could have been— more futile, trivial, foolish than the first sproutings of the Romantic Movement in sham ballads, sham spectres, sham Gothic ruins; the Movement which flowered gloriously so soon after into such a richness of scent and colour? And remember—'

(Hold back thy waves, Alpheus! for the dread voice has not done speaking.)

'Remember that whenever man, in his fury of mad action, his kicking up the dust of this patient planet, has paused for a moment to look within himself, what life-transmuting, world-transforming secrets he has found! Remember Buddha, Christ, St. Augustine, Thomas à Kempis and Montaigne and Wordsworth, and how by the discovery of reverie, Rousseau enriched the world with a strange and new beauty? What pages of modern prose would you have rather written than those in Rousseau's fifth Promenade in which he describes the reveries of his sojourn on that Swiss island? Remember Sir Thomas Browne's admonition, "Despise not the obliquities of younger ways, nor despair of better things whereof there is yet no prospect"; and, my dear sir, don't talk yourself into an old fogey before your time!'

XI

I have dwelt at length on Shakespeare's gift for character-creation, because in this aspect of his art he has no rival. In his creation of souls as he had no predecessor (with one august Exception, and even Adam and Eve are more 'types' than characters, being quite unlike Hamlet and Cleopatra), so no one ever since has been his equal. He was the first portrayer of the subtleties of the spirit, and he makes us aware of these subtleties by embodying them in the accents, rhythms and overtones of expressive speech.

But why, we may ask ourselves, should this be so overwhelming an achievement; why should this creation of crowds of people have an esthetic value so astonishing that all other values seem to grow dim beside it? Most of us rather dislike people, especially in crowds. Sir Walter Raleigh's lines,

> *I wish I loved the Human Race;*
> *I wish I loved its silly face;*
> *I wish I liked the way it walks,*
> *I wish I liked the way it talks;*

And when I'm introduced to one
I wish I thought what Jolly Fun!

These lines, wrung from Sir Walter's heart at an Oxford garden-party, probably express what is most kindly in our feelings when we meet in crowds our fellow human beings. Why then should we think it such 'Jolly Fun,' and taste so fierce an ecstasy, on being introduced to them in books, and even rejoice in encountering bores in novels whom, in life, we would walk so many miles to avoid? Is it not because life itself is in itself an end, and has no other end, and that the fullest, most intense and idiosyncratic spirit of life, such as animates the living characters in plays and novels, where we are free from all tiresome devitalizing relations with them, is for us on this earth the most fascinating of cosmic phenomena, however slight an interest it may arouse in the other stars?

'Life is a pure flame,' Sir Thomas Browne wrote, 'and we live by an invisible Sun within us'; and just as those places and epochs—Athens in the time of Pericles, Florence at the renascence, the London of Queen Elizabeth, the Paris of the *Roi-Soleil*, which have been richest in revealed personalities, and in which the flame of life has blazed in the most varied constellations—just as in these places and epochs the purpose of creation (as far as we can see that it has a purpose), has seemed to reach its most supreme achievement, so are not those writers who create the greatest variety of human spirits, or those painters or musicians who express the finest essence of their own fine spirits in their works, worthy of the praise we give them?

This effect of life, life in all its brilliance, its oceanic amplitude and variety, the creation of a whole world of vivid human beings, is, after his power of purely poetic evocation, the product, then, of the next great gift of Shakespeare, whose development we witness as we glance from the comic characters in the background of his early plays to the superhuman beings who fill the stage of his later tragedies. And not only are these early figures feeble and pale in character-drawing, but the comedies in which they figure show no great depth or serious artistic purpose—show little more, indeed, than Shakespeare's wit and cleverness in the use of language, and his flexible eagerness to adapt himself to the taste of the moment. But, comparing these early comedies with those produced in the growing maturity of his genius, what a development we witness, not only in character-creation, but in thought and feeling! If we place Feste side by side with Speed, Dull by Dogberry, and listen to the divine converse of Beatrice and Benedick after the tit-tat of Rosaline and Biron in *Love's Labour's Lost*, our sense of the beauty, energy and power of these later plays is a measure of the distance we have travelled in so brief a space of time. And then, after another few years, the pastoral scene in *The Winter's Tale* shows us Shakespeare's comedy transmuted at last into something so exquisite, and touched by so

divine a beauty, that even our arid eyes are almost suf-
fused by unaccustomed tears.[17]

XII

And if we read the historical plays in the order of
their composition, we are aware again of the same stu-
pendous stride of genius. The four earliest of these, the
three *Henry VI* plays and *Richard III*, are what the
Patriot King called 'stuff'; they are woven of the stuff of
the common Elizabethan drama, and whether Shakespeare really wrote them has been often doubted. And
yet from my reading of these four plays I remember a
few scenes which I feel he must have written—a few
gleams through the morning mists from the 'glory hereafter to be revealed,' from the sun still below the hori-
zon, of his ascending genius. Touched by these gleams
of dawn, I see looming faintly, to borrow his own
words,

> *The baby figure of the giant mass*
> *Of things to come at large.*

In the musings of the poor mild King in the third
Henry VI play, on the happiness of the shepherd's lot

[17] In his essay on *The Tempest* Professor Stoll suggests that it is
mainly the beauty of this scene, along with the dirge in *Cymbeline*,
and Prospero's speech on the 'Cloud-capp'd Towers' in *The Tempest*
which has given rise to the beautiful 'out of The Depths, on to the
Height' view of Shakespeare's last three plays, which really contain
plenty of ugliness, cynicism, horror and grossness.

(II, v) we find a soliloquy and a poetic daydream that no one but Shakespeare could have written, and in the death of Cardinal Beaufort (*II Hen. VI*, III, iii) the note of Shakespearean tragedy is first sounded in that scene of despair and dreadful death. Cade in this play is almost a living figure, and even more alive is his derisive follower, Smith 'the weaver,' who, when Cade tells Sir Humphrey Stafford that his father was of royal blood, though stolen at birth and trained as a bricklayer, Smith ironically confirms this boast by declaring, 'Sir, he made a chimney in my father's house, and the bricks are alive at this day to testify it; therefore deny it not' (IV, ii).

The Second Murderer of Clarence in *Richard III* also comes to life when he complains before the murder of his attack of conscience, adding cheerfully, however, that this 'holy humour' was not apt to last longer than it took him to count twenty (I, iv).

In the terrible dream of Clarence of this scene the authentic note of tragedy is again touched, and finds utterance in the first passages of great poetry, which, with the strangely beautiful opening line of the drama,

Now is the winter of our discontent,

are the earliest touches of magical evocation to be found in these historical plays. Clarence describes how his drowning soul could not escape from the sea depths, 'To find the empty, vast, and wandering air,' and how, when he had passed the melancholy flood into the

'Kingdom of perpetual night,' the first that met him was the ghost of Warwick (listen! for we hear Shakespeare's footstep), who cried aloud,

> *'What scourge for perjury*
> *Can this dark monarchy afford false Clarence?'*
> *And so he vanish'd: then came wandering by*
> *A shadow like an angel, with bright hair*
> *Dabbl'd in blood; and he shriek'd out aloud,*
> *'Clarence is come,—false, fleeting, perjur'd Clarence.'*

However, in spite of these touches, we must agree with Sir Edmund Chambers that in these four plays 'you shall hardly trace the lineaments of the creator of Macbeth and Iago in those of the youngest and most brilliant graduate in the school of Marlowe and Kyd.' They were written, the same critic adds, 'while the golden key to the unexplored gardens of enchantment which he was to make his own had still to be found.' [18]

When Shakespeare came to write *King John*, however, the key was in his hand, the gateway into his kingdom is pushed a little open. The Bastard is not only full of vitality, he is Shakespeare's first fully-alive creation, and he plays an important part in the play. Shakespeare's gift of pathos first shows itself in the heart-rending scene between Hubert and the young Arthur, and in the great laments of Constance, and, as always, the awakening of his great gifts awakens his great poetic power.

[18] *Shakespeare: a Survey*, p. 10.

> *Of Nature's gifts thou mayst with lilies boast*
> *And with the half-blown rose.*

(Bother that 'half-blown rose'! Its beauty blurs my eyes, and I can hardly go on quoting.)

> *Grief fills the room up of my absent child,*
> *Lies in his bed, walks up and down with me,*
> *Puts on his pretty looks—*

(Where's my handkerchief? I can quote no more.)

In this play of *King John* we find the terrifying evidence of Shakespeare's tragic power in that scene where in brief heavy whispers King John tempts Hubert to the murder of Prince Arthur (III, iii):

K. JOHN.	*Death.*
HUBERT.	*My Lord?*
K. JOHN.	*A grave.*
HUBERT.	*He shall not live.*
K. JOHN.	*Enough.*

In this scene Shakespeare, as Swinburne says, 'sounds a deeper note and touches a subtler string in the tragic nature of man than had been struck by any poet save Dante alone, since the region of the Greek tragedians.' When in the same play (IV, iii), Salisbury declares that he and his peers will no longer

> *attend the foot*
> *That leaves the print of blood where'er it walks,*

we hear the tread of Shakespeare in a phrase even more terrible than Macbeth's as he approaches Duncan's chamber,

> *Thou sure and firm-set earth,*
> *Hear not my steps, which way they walk.*

But *King John* is still a play of incoherent patchwork, and most of it is poor enough. But in *Richard II* Shakespeare fully emerges from the veil of stuff which had hid his figure; the sun of his genius bursts through the mists and shines forth in full morning illumination. He writes an historical play in that early lyric manner which is all his own, that style in which he wrote at the same date the lyric tragedy of *Romeo and Juliet*, and the lyric comedy of the *Midsummer Night*. The play is a tragedy of pity, pity for the passionate weakness of the lovely, ineffectual King. It might well be set to music, as Sir Edmund Chambers suggests, and form the libretto of an opera; Richard's own part being, after the wheel of fortune has begun to carry him downwards, 'one long and elaborated recitative of profound and subtle pathos.' And what a flood of poetry wells up in this play, as in Shakespeare's other play of this year, *A Midsummer Night's Dream*. What enchantment when Richard says, gazing in a mirror at the scene of his dethronement,

> *A brittle glory shineth in this face:*
> *As brittle as the glory is the face,*

or in his other lines,

> *For God's sake, let us sit upon the ground*
> *And tell sad stories of the death of Kings.*

> *My large kingdom for a little grave,*
> *A little little grave—*

Shakespeare's golden key has touched the lips of almost all the characters in this play, as when one of the King's uncles, 'Old John of Gaunt, time-honoured Lancaster,' gives lyric utterance to his love for England,

> *This little world,*
> *This precious stone set in the silver sea,*

and York, his other uncle, sings amid the sad troubles of the time,

> *Comfort's in heaven; and we are on the earth,—*

and even a dummy bishop chants a splendid dirge for the banished Norfolk,

> *Many a time hath banish'd Norfolk fought*
> *For Jesu Christ in glorious Christian field,*
> *Streaming the ensign of the Christian cross*
> *Against black pagans, Turks, and Saracens;*
> *And toil'd with works of war, retired himself*
> *To Italy; and there at Venice gave*
> *His body to that pleasant country's earth,*
> *And his pure soul unto his Captain Christ,*
> *Under whose colours he had fought so long.*

In this play, as in *The Merchant of Venice*, the most living characters play the most important parts; and in the next of the historical series, the *Henry IV* plays, a great gross immortal creature, a monster of vitality, rushes in and absorbs the interest, while the historical characters and interests fade away, as it has been well said, into a dim background of discoloured tapestry.

And again when we compare those tragedies of circumstances in the historical plays and in *Romeo and Juliet*, tragedies of failure in the mastery of events and things, with the dreadful tragedies of the soul in the later plays, we are aware of an even more vertiginous advance. A sense of the awful and enigmatic quality of life darkens these tragedies, in which, as Dr. Bradley says, the forces that meet us 'stretch far beyond the little group of figures and the tiny tract of space and time in which they appear. The darkness that covers the scene, and the light that strikes across it, are more than our common night and day.' This growing intensity of emotion, this immense scope of Shakespeare's genius in the worlds of passion and power he creates, and still vaster worlds of thought—the whole literary and psychological content of his greatest plays gives us the impression of the development of a demonic, supernatural gift. In passing from the tragedy of Lucretia's pedantic rape, with her long, frigid, and high-conceited declamations against Night, Opportunity and Time, to the tragedy of Lear's madness, we have travelled the distance from one star to another.

THE ENIGMAS

Chapter V

THE ENIGMAS

THE QUESTION whether this gigantic advance of Shakespeare's tragic power is due, as the romantic critics say, to a tragic experience of his spirit, or was the result, as his hard-boiled biographers maintain, of nothing more than his alertness in complying with the taste (now turning to tragedy) of the public, this is the first of the three great Shakespearean enigmas which I have spoken of already, and one which has nonplussed the brains of all those who have tried to solve it. The ascertainment of the approximate chronological order in which Shakespeare wrote his plays has for many of his critics, by suggesting a mysterious Dark Period in his life, bewildered them into depicting this actor-manager and purveyor for the public taste as an enormously sentimental person, who made use of his sonnets and tragedies to display to the world the pageant of a broken heart. But do not his realist biographers, who abhor and reject this kind of interpretation, show symptoms, in their matter-of-fact explanations, of an equally grave delirium? When Sir Sidney Lee, one of the most matter-of-fact of all the hard-boiled Shakespeare critics, writes of Shakespeare, 'his literary attainments and successes were chiefly valued as serving the prosaic end of making a permanent provision for himself and his daughters,' and says that 'the sole biographical inference deducible from the Sonnets is that' at one time in his career Shakespeare disdained no weapon of flattery in an endeavour to monopolise the bountiful patronage of a young man of rank, does he not also rave, though in more prosaic accents, as much as the maddest sentimentalist and blatherskite of them all?

II

Of another aspect of the development of Shakespeare's genius I am not competent to speak. Step by step—and his strides are the strides of a giant—he became the greatest master of the stage the world has ever seen. He added all the resources of stagecraft and theatrical effect to his repertory, and he used them with unfailing sureness, and, we may also say, without the slightest scruple. His comedies are based on theatrical disguises, his tragedies take place within the framework of the most sensational melodramas; they were written for the stage, and undoubtedly, as Mr. Granville-Barker has pointed out, there are scenes in them, like the mock-trial by means of stools in *Lear*, for instance (III, vi), whose dramatic value can only be appreciated when we see them acted. We gain something, we gain much, by witnessing the stage-performance of Shakespeare's plays, with their scenes of fear and horror which make us hold our breath; but heavens, what we lose—at least, what I lose—by this kind of soul-exposure! Save for a boyhood's memory of Salvini as Othello, no representation of a Shakespeare play has ever enriched—has ever done anything but tarnish and degrade—my sense of its significance and beauty. Shakespeare's tragedies are dreadful, but no tragedy can equal the tragedy of seeing one of them performed. What actor with his robust acting, what actress with her display of female charm, can do anything but caricature and make grotesque those inhabitants of the world of poetry who, in our imagination, lead their immortal life apart? One howl of English declamation, heard across the ether, is almost enough to make me pack up my bag and leave for ever the shores of my adopted land. Then, too, the theatrical frames of Shakespeare's farcical or melodramatic plots become much too prominent and engross too much attention when we see them acted; the disharmony between plot and character becomes grossly apparent; and what people are really is obscured for us by the unreal things they do.[1]

[1] The dramatic critic, A. B. Walkley, in an essay on *Measure for Measure*, after speaking of the poetry of the play, which to the reader seems so marvellous, and the great meditations on Life and Death and Love and Purity on which the reader's mind can dwell, adds, 'In the theatre, of course, no such process of selection is possible. The childishness of the plot is thrust under our noses, and the absolutely idiotic behaviour of the Duke is, so to speak, rubbed into us. Then the jack-pudding nonsense of Pompey and the appalling tiresomeness of Elbow, and the wishywashy japes of Lucio must be doggedly endured' (A. B. Walkley, *Drama and Life*, p. 156). It is only fair, however, to add that the author notes two great scenes in the play which profit immensely by stage-representation, 'the first where Isabella turns with rage and loathing

So turning tail from the first of the Theban monsters
I have mentioned, the dark problem of the Dark Period
(that problem I leave with the Sonnets to other cranks),
I now find myself face to face with monster number
two—the problem of the stage-representation of Shakespeare's plays. I am, of course, aware that there are
people of the most delicate sensibility who love to see
Shakespeare's plays acted; but I cannot enter into their
minds, nor understand their taste, any more than I can
understand the taste of people who dislike oysters or
cannot read Jane Austen. There is a gulf between us;
and into the gulfs that so dreadfully yawn between
people who share many fine tastes together, it is best
not to peer;—best it is to shudder and pass on. I at least
am not alone in my preference for reading Shakespeare's
plays to seeing them performed. It is shared by many
of his wisest lovers, and Goethe, Hazlitt, Lamb and
Coleridge, were all of this opinion. Coleridge declared
that he could not witness a Shakespearean performance
without 'pain, disgust and indignation,' and is reported
to have said that all such performances should be for-
bidden by Act of Parliament. Lamb's essay *On the
Tragedies of Shakespeare, Considered with Reference
to their fitness for stage Representation,* is the classical
statement of this point of view.[2]

---

on Angelo (II, iv), and the still greater scene (III, i) of her
dismay and total bouleversement when she finds that her brother
clings more to his own life than to his sister's honour' (*Ibid.*, p.
158).

[2] Lamb was a great play-goer and lover of the actor's art, but it

III

And yet it certainly does sound preposterous, as Professor Stoll points out, for those who love Shakespeare's drama to peer only through their spectacles at its text; to shudder at seeing it acted, and to maintain that the fulness of its dramatic effect is thwarted and counteracted by the only means of securing that effect which ever, for a moment, occupied Shakespeare's thoughts.

Having read so much sentimental tosh about Shake-

---

hurt and grieved him to see Shakespeare's plays acted; they were less calculated for performance on a stage, he said, than the plays of any dramatist soever. Their distinguishing excellence is the reason that they should be so, for they are charged with an intellectual and imaginative content which eludes the stage, and must elude it, since no 'low tricks upon the eye and ear'—the body's eye which is so importunate, and its ear so deaf to the beauty of spoken verse—can conceive or present these treasures of the mind. Seeing, he declares, 'is not believing, the actual sight destroys the faith'; it is only in the 'beautiful compromise' that we make in reading, in what we see with the mind's eye, and listen to with its ear, that we can appreciate those states of the soul, those dreams of the imagination which Shakespeare at his best depicts. Such fine visions cannot be materialized in wretched flesh and blood without being sullied and turned from their very nature.

J. M. Robertson (a critic with whom I generally find myself in furious disagreement) accepts and corroborates Lamb's conclusions in a fine essay which is printed in the *Homage to Shakespeare* (pp. 141-5). Lamb's essay, he says, has been denied and contradicted, but as far as he knew, it had never been answered. What Lamb called his paradox, is, Mr. Robertson declares, a paradox in the proper sense of the word, a proposition that seems false, but is true. He finds it true 'that the admittedly greatest of all dramatists was not rightly or essentially a dramatist but something else; and that the end at which he certainly aimed throughout his life is not speare (and I have read oceans) I find it a kind of satisfaction to come now and then on a solid piece of none-of-your-nonsense criticism like that of Professor Stoll; it is a rock, a firm anchorage in the tepid sea of gush. All the same, being by nature, by bringing up and by preference, soft-boiled, romantic, and full of soul, I do not mean to let myself be trampled on without a feeble squirm or two; so turning (as worms will) on the professor from Minnesota, I shall try to face, not once more the question of stage-performance, which other writers have raised as well as he, but the problem pro-

---

the end which he best achieves'; the true paradox of Shakespeare being, he repeats, 'that of the master poet led by economic destiny to the work in which alone, to an end he could not have foreseen, his poetic power could attain its supremest possibilities—that task, which, if economically free, he would probably not have chosen, of being the poetic mouthpiece of a world of imagined men and women.'

As a confirmation of this thesis, Mr. Robertson says that while Shakespeare is coming to be read more and more every year, his plays are less often acted, and fewer and fewer of them are being put upon the stage. The German boast that Shakespeare is so much more frequently acted in Germany than in England should in no way disconcert us, since it is simply a proof of how little the Germans really appreciate or understand Shakespeare.

How, I ask you, are stage-enthusiasts—I ask you, Granville-Barker, and you, too, Desmond MacCarthy, and you, Maurice Baring, going to answer Robertson, Charles Lamb, Hazlitt, Coleridge, Goethe and me? It is really up to you to make a reply; and such a reply to be valid should, I suggest, enumerate first of all the scenes in Shakespeare's plays which are only effective upon the stage, and secondly a record of concrete esthetic experiences, of the rendering of Shakespearean rôles by great actors and actresses by which the imaginative impression of these rôles has been deepened and enriched.

pounded by that third growling Theban monster, which, ever since he led it by the nose into the arena, has dogged my footsteps and kept me in a state of funk. How can you pretend, so yelps the creature, to understand Shakespeare's plays or appreciate their merits, unless you see them and only see them, by the light in which he wrote them, and in which his contemporaries, for whom alone he wrote, witnessed their performance?

Well, first of all, let me at once admit that it is undoubtedly true, and most important to be said, that a great part of Shakespeare, and almost the whole of the Elizabethan drama, can best be understood by the study of the drama of that time.

But now—suddenly, without warning—I make a big face at the formidable creature; I turn on that riddling Sphinx with a riddle of my own. What explanation can *you* give, I demand with emphasis, how do you account for the difference, the great gulf without a bottom, between Shakespeare and the other Elizabethans—between indeed what is good and what is bad in Shakespeare himself? How do you explain, I ask, the fact that, while almost all the stuff of the Elizabethan drama has become long since obsolete, musty and moth-eaten, and is never read except by special students, all this time Shakespeare's great plays are growing, and have for centuries been growing, in renown, significance and importance, not only in England, but all over the world?

Why, at the three-hundredth anniversary of his death, were tributes of passion and adoration, sent to celebrate it from all over Europe,—North and South America; why did Brahmin, Muslim, Egyptian, Burmese, Japanese and Chinese poets, the inhabitants of Iceland, the negroes of South Africa, 'the scalded Indian, and the poor boy that shakes at the foot of the Riphean hills,' why did they all burst into song, and raise the vast babel of their discordant voices to hymn his praise? [3] Why, for instance—to put in more moderate terms my query—are Shakespeare's Roman plays read and re-read and still acted, while those of Ben Jonson, once so much more famous, have been long since half forgotten? Why do people all over the world read *Hamlet*, translate it, and write books about it, while no one, even in England, gives a glance at Kyd's *Spanish Tragedy*, or any of those more popular revenge-plays of the time, with which you class it? If it is only the contemporaries of a writer who really understand and appreciate his merits, then surely those among his works they admired most must be his best achievements, and the extremely popular *Titus Adronicus*, and *Richard III*, which were several times reprinted, must rank far above plays like *Macbeth* and *The Tempest*, whose survival is only due to their inclusion in the Folio seven years after Shakespeare's death?

Granted that Shakespeare took the stock characters of the stage and put its stock sentiments into their mouths, what else did he put there which endows them with an inalienable reality and makes them live for ever

[3] See *A Book of Homage to Shakespeare* (Milford, 1916).

in the imagination? An individuality of utterance, a
tone, a rhythm, a cadence for each voice, you say. But
is not just that personal, characteristic voice, expressive
as it is of inner moods and ways of feeling, the very
thing that makes a person most himself? Is not Song,
as Carlyle said, the very central essence of a human
being, and all the rest but wrappings and hulls? If then,
unlike all the other dramatic writers of the world,
Shakespeare could make his old ghosts sing, and each
of them sing in a voice that is his alone, what can matter to us the irrelevant, theatrical, unmotived, melodramatic things which they are compelled by the plots
in which they appear to do? And all those worlds of
thought, dream and imagination, those realms of passion and felicity, those happier islands, those 'palaces
echoing with dance and song,' which he created, and
which have become, and are becoming more and more
places of happy refuge for the human spirit,—do you
mean to say that Shakespeare had no notion of their
immortal fabric, and was actually so stupid that he never
saw the meaning of what he wrote? [4]

So defying this and all other Sphinxes, I persist in
reading Shakespeare's plays with my own intelligence,

[4] It is only fair to say that Professor Stoll in his latest publications, *Poets and Playwrights* (University of Minnesota Press, 1930),
and his essay on *The Tempest* which I have already mentioned,
provides himself a most eloquent answer to this question. Wearying,
apparently, of attacking other Shakespeare idolaters, he exposes his
well-grounded reasons for an admiration of Shakespeare—one might
almost say a worship—of his own.

and in witnessing their performance in the theatre of my own imagination, lit as it is by the light of lamps far different from those which glared before the stage. It was for the Globe Theatre, of course, that he wrote them; 'his great soul,' as Carlyle says, 'had to crush itself, as best it could, into that and no other mould.' Or, as we may more prosaically paraphrase these terms of hero-worship, he chose the drama as the dominant and most lucrative form of the literature of his age. This was his instrument of expression, and probably, as his poems suggest, the only instrument by which his gifts could have found their full expression, though there is reason to suppose that, could he have afforded it, he would much rather have been a writer of poems than a playwright. But though the drama was the instrument which drew forth his gifts, his genius gradually outgrew that instrument, and we can best appreciate that genius when we can emancipate it, as by reading we can emancipate it, from the kind of drama in which his contemporaries delighted, and with which he provided them without stint.

But true drama, in the highest sense of the word, drama which does not rely on histrionic effects, on the weaving and unweaving of plots, and hardly, except in a formal sense, on action, but rather in the presentation of characters and the dramatic clashes between them, or in the conflict of tragic forces in great souls, leading to terrible conclusions—it is in this kind of drama that Shakespeare's highest achievement consists. And this can be best appreciated by reading Shakespeare's plays for their texture rather than for their structure. Scenes like the meeting of Macbeth with Lady Macbeth after Duncan's murder, of Othello's dreadful conversation with Iago, or Claudio's talk with Isabella, or that marvellous interview between Brutus and Cassius, in which Coleridge found the most convincing proof of Shakespeare's superhuman genius—it is scenes like these, where the dramatic tension between two great characters is so poignantly portrayed, which make us understand what Goethe meant when he declared that he had often said, and would often say again, that dramatic poetry was of all human achievements the crown and consummation.

IV

When, therefore, I have dipped my cup in the pot of the greatest pot-boiler the world has ever known, these two elements—pure poetry, and dramatic poetry —in the sense which Goethe used the word, are the most heady ingredients of the draught I sip. Whether the pure poetry of the earlier plays—those passages which come to us like 'parcels of the purest sky,' like splendour out of heaven, or the thrilling experience in the later dramas of a life tenser, more vivid than our own—which of these two ingredients I find the more intoxicating it would be difficult to say.

There are other elements, too, in this draught of Shakespeare's brewing—in the potent wine that came

to fill at last the great jewelled cup of words he fashioned, to drink from which is one of the most wonderful experiences life affords. One element winking at
the brim is, of course, Shakespeare's humour—for he
alone, among all the great poets of the world, possessed
the gift of humour—a teeming, comic imagination and
inexhaustible fountain of sparkling geniality and fun.
All critics mention this; but there is another and amazing aspect of his achievement, about which, since I
have seen no mention of it, I should like to say a word
or two.

In the work of all other dramatic writers, in Æschylus
and Sophocles and Racine (and also, indeed, in all the
great novelists), we find a certain uniformity of tone,
and, so to speak, only one subject; a scene or character
from one of their works might appear without any
shock to our sense of tone in any of the others. But
Shakespeare was the master of many styles, and each of
his great plays possesses its own atmosphere and colour.
Even in the two fairy plays, the silvery moonlight of
the *Dream* is very different from the faint haze of
enchantment which envelops *The Tempest*, and every
one of the tragedies differs from all the others. *Romeo
and Juliet* glows with the richness of Giorgione; the
atmosphere of *Lear* is, as Dr. Bradley says, cold and
dark, and envelops its dim-lit scenes with a kind of a
winter mist: it would be impossible to imagine a scene
like the cliff-scene transferred from *Lear* into the glare
of *Othello*; while to pass from *Julius Cæsar* to *Antony*

and Cleopatra is like passing from a gallery of antique sculpture to a great palace rich with Titian's or Paul Veronese's frescoes. That the painter of one of these scenes should be the painter of the others seems a constantly repeated marvel; if we should find that the pictures of Giorgione, Raphael, Michelangelo, of Titian or Veronese, had all been painted by one hand, we could hardly be more astonished.

v

I wonder if any of my readers supposes for a moment that I am pleased with the pallid words which have been dripping from my pen? I am not pleased with them; and should like permission to dip that pen just for once into the purple ink which fills my elderly inkpot.

And, Lord, what fun it is to splash that ink about!

I promise not to offend for long the modern meagre indigestion, the modern distaste for the beauty and choice of words; and if my attempt to write finely on my fine subject turns any reader's stomach, let him turn the page. I shall, therefore, with (or without) permission have recourse to that small section of our vocabulary which contains a group of exquisite new-formed words, words which, many of them, have been minted by poets from the name of another poet, and into which, as into a flask of crystal, they have distilled as it were the nectar, the fragrance, the quintessence of his soul, 'the purest efficacy and extraction' (I cannot forgo the pleasure of quoting these perhaps too-familiar phrases) 'the precious life-blood of a master-spirit, embalmed and treasured up on purpose to a life beyond life.'

If, holding our breath a moment, we allow one of these 'essential' words (for each contains an essence), 'Sophoclean,' 'Virgilian,' 'Miltonic' to quiver and shine before us like a bubble of the air—like Milton's 'airy shell' in which 'sweet echo' dwelt unseen—each will glimmer with a jewel-like colour of its own, each ring and chime with its own note and overtones of music.

Let us then make a trial of this evocation of essences by means of words, let us pronounce the Keatsean vocable 'Shakespearean' (for it comes from Keats' golden mint), and watch the response it awakens in us. What are the precipitates of appreciation which have been deposited, film by opalescent film, in that delicate, resounding shell, with what far-off ocean-ripples of perennial applause does it murmur, faintly?

All the other vocables of this class, 'Horatian,' 'Virgilian,' 'Dantesque,' 'Miltonic,' have but one tint, and ring with only one tone, since these poets have sounded but one note clear and distinct enough to impress the world with the need of a word to denote it; but the 'giant mass' of Shakespeare is so many-sided, and presents such varied mountain-aspects, each reverberating with its own echoes, that this vocable is rich with various meanings. It suggests first of all that open-air breadth of sunlit vision, that cheerful all-comprehending sympathy with the feelings and ways of men, which was Fitz-Gerald's meaning when he wrote of the 'broad Shakespearean daylight' diffused over the novels of Sir Walter Scott.

The word is also used to describe that mingling of pathos and comedy in which Shakespeare is without a rival, and of which Lear's colloquies with his Fool, and Mrs. Quickly's description of Falstaff's death, are among the most famous examples. 'After I saw him fumble with the sheets and play with flowers and smile upon his fingers' ends, I knew there was but one way; for his nose was as sharp as a pen, and a' babbled of green fields. "How now, Sir John!" quoth I: "what man! be of good cheer." So a' cried out "God, God, God!" three or four times: now I, to comfort him, bid him a' should not think of God, I hoped there was no need to trouble himself with any such thoughts yet' (*Henry V*, II, iii).

This is Shakespearean; and even more so the awakening of Lear after his madness (IV, vii), which is regarded by modern opinion as perhaps the greatest of all Shakespeare's achievements.

And finally a deeper hue dyes this jewel-tinted word; the airy shell echoes with a music more solemn than that of songs and sighs and laughter. This dark stain, this far-off sound, 'swinging slow with sullen roar,' comes to us from the dreadful histories and dooms of great characters caught in the web of Destiny; wrecked by some flaw in themselves, or rendered helpless amid a crushing environment of evil, and swept down by terrible, non-human forces on the remorseless flood of fate. Othello, Lear, Coriolanus, Macbeth are supremely great Shakespearean figures; and when we are told that of all the personages of the placid eighteenth century the figure of Swift, and perhaps that of Dr. Johnson, with his almost insane fear of death, are perhaps the only ones which might possibly be called Shakespearean in this tragic sense, we feel that in the statement there is an element of truth. And finally there are those Shakespearean scenes in which terror and strangeness are added to tragic beauty.

Shakespeare's supremacy shines out in almost everything that he undertakes in the maturity of his genius, but it is in scenes like these that the immensity, the unmeasurability of that pre-eminence daunts the imagination. The imperious eagle has soared beyond our wonder; the giant mass, whose upheaval we have witnessed, has risen above the mists that veiled it and touches the sky. So now in this adjective voices shrill with fear or hushed in horror echo; and supernatural voices reach our ears: 'Murder most foul!' 'Hamlet, remember!' 'Sleep no more! Macbeth hath murdered sleep.'

Of all of Shakespeare's plays, *Macbeth* is the most Shakespearean in this more sombre meaning of the epithet, and in the word 'Macbeth' as we evoke it, we see the splash of blood; dreadful shapes appear and flicker, dimly, as in dim crystal-gazing; Macbeth steals to Duncan's chamber, the inexplicable Third Murderer silently draws near the scene of murder; Banquo's ghost sits at the feast, shaking his gory locks in silence, and Lady Macbeth moves and mutters in her sleep.

THE TOUCH BEYOND

Chapter VI

THE TOUCH BEYOND

A<small>ND YET</small> from my last reperusal of Shakespeare's plays there remains something more—there is still a touch beyond. Like all wise readers, my pleasure in a good book is greatly enhanced by my sense of companionship with its author. The older I grow, the more I love this affable intercourse with the fair-spoken friend behind the book I read, with Montaigne behind his essays, or with Sir Walter Scott as he writes his novels. But how on earth is one to establish any sort of human relationship with Shakespeare? For the hero of Carlyle's *Hero Worship* I have no great liking, nor is the official all-British Shakespeare and Empire-builder a friend for me. The demi-god, the enthroned divinity of the romantic critics, impeccable, supernaturally inspired, and with a mind out-topping knowledge, I cannot believe in, and equally incredible I find the Shakespeare which his modern, hard-boiled biographers portray, a man, as it were, outside humanity, a kind of monster, who did not think or feel the things he wrote, but turned out the sublimest poetry and the grossest ribaldry merely in the way of business. Must I then stand glaring at that Inconceivability with white lips in open-mouthed amazement, my eyes starting from my head? Is 'stupefaction' the only word to describe my state of mind when, face to face with Shakespeare's achievement, I try to imagine what sort of man Shakespeare really was? Hadn't I better just sit down in silence and quietly go mad?

II

Into the select circle of professors and scholars, as they were discussing in hushed voices the appalling problem, there burst, not many years ago, the outrageous figure of a loud journalist and shameless pornographic writer with a new interpretation that shed a new and surprising light upon the subject. Mr. Bernard Shaw has well described the shocking comedy of this scandal. To write a new book on Shakespeare, Mr. Shaw explains, great refinement and delicacy of taste were considered necessary, and combined with this profound scholarship, high academic distinction, or at least an assured literary reputation. 'Now,' he adds, 'if there is a man on earth who is the utter contrary of everything that this description implies; whose very existence is an insult to the ideal it realizes; whose eye disparages, whose resonant voice denounces, whose cold shoulder jostles every decency, every delicacy, every amenity, every dignity, every sweet usage of that quiet life of mutual admiration in which perfect appreciation of Shakespeare is expected to arise, that man is Frank Harris.' And yet the contribution made to the interpretation of Shakespeare by Frank Harris [1] is of considerable importance, and has greatly influenced subsequent critics. 'They will first crab you,' as Mr. Desmond MacCarthy wrote to Harris, 'then crib you'; and this forecast has proved a true one, for Harris's name is not mentioned, save in disparagement, I believe, in the writing of any of the Shakespearean scholars who have profited by his book, except in that of the greatest of them all, Dr. Bradley.[2]

Contrary to the received opinion that Shakespeare did not reveal himself in his plays, Frank Harris maintains that he did so, not once, but again and again. After

[1] *The Man Shakespeare*, Frank Palmer, 1909.

[2] 'A good many of Mr. Harris's views I cannot share, and I had arrived at almost all the ideas expressed in my lecture . . . before reading his papers. But I found in them also valuable ideas which were quite new to me and would probably be so to many readers' (*Oxford Lectures on Poetry*, 1920, p. 315). Dr. Bradley is writing of Frank Harris's first exposition of his views in some articles published in the *Saturday Review*, in 1898; it was a great pity, he said, that the articles were not collected and published in a book. When, however, this book was published, Dr. Bradley added to this earlier note: 'Mr. Harris has published, in *The Man Shakespeare*, the substance of the articles, and also matter which, in my judgment, has much less value.' If the original note seems somewhat grudging, Dr. Bradley's addition to it is the mildest of understatements, for after about sixty pages of subtle and original interpretation, the mania for finding in Shakespeare's plays the story of his inner life seizes hold of Frank Harris, as it seized hold of Samuel Butler, and so many writers on the subject, leading them to the maddest and most grotesque conclusions. In this latter part of his book, however, Harris has the courage to say one thing which no other critics have liked to mention—the fact, namely, that if any deductions are to be made from Shakespeare's writings about his nature, an excessive and almost morbid sensuality must have been part of his endowment.

reading and re-reading them many times, he became aware, he tells us, of a certain unity underlying all the diversity of Shakespeare's characters. 'And, at length,' he adds, 'out of the myriad voices in the plays, I began to hear more and more insistent the accents of one voice, and out of the crowd of faces began to distinguish more and more clearly the features of the writer.' This voice and this face were, to put it briefly, Hamlet's face and voice; in Hamlet, Shakespeare, he said, had portrayed his own soul, the very essence of his nature; and when he wrote Hamlet's speeches, it was his own heart he was writing down.[3] This is made plain, in the first place, Frank Harris says, by the fact that when Shakespeare's characters fall, as they so often fall, out of character, and say things which such personages would never say, they are very apt to drop into Hamlet's way of talking —to think his thoughts and express them in his language. Shakespeare portrays, moreover, not once, but many times, figures that resemble Hamlet, dreamy contemplative beings given to irony and melancholy brooding. Romeo is the first of these; and Romeo, as Hazlitt said, is Hamlet in love. He is, indeed, Hamlet's young brother, less mature and less complex, but absent-minded like the student-prince, and living, like him, in a world of his own imagination. Richard II, in the

[3] The possible resemblance between Hamlet and Shakespeare himself had been more than once suggested before Harris, but only in a cursory way. Harris was the first to develop it fully in all its implications.

play of about this date, is another Hamlet, a passive contemplator, rather than a master, of his fate. A more mature character of this cast is Jaques, whom Shakespeare added to the figures in the old story from which his later play, *As You Like It*, is derived. Jaques, who finds that all the world's a stage, possesses Hamlet's detachment, his wit, and his lightning-like intelligence, and is, like him, wrapped up in a humorous sadness of his own.

Much of Hamlet, too, is to be found in the exiled Duke of this play, and still more in the 'old fantastical Duke of dark corners' in *Measure for Measure*, with his love for lonely contemplation and the life removed. His great speech to Claudio in prison, 'Reason thus with life' (III, i), so apparently callous when addressed to one condemned to death, is an instance of a Shakespearean character who forgets dramatic propriety to indulge in Hamlet-like meditations on life and the problems of human destiny.

In Feste and Touchstone, and Shakespeare's other clowns, with their ironic detachment like Hamlet's and their wit like his, touching melancholy with a sting of absurdity, turning life inside out and upside down with their disintegrating phrases, again we find the Hamlet who could outclown the gravediggers in their confabulation. Of Prospero in Shakespeare's last play it is hardly necessary to speak, so plainly is he an incarnation of Hamlet's spirit. Indeed in the whole progress of Shakespeare's plays we notice how more and more men of action and resolution tend to be replaced by dreaming and brooding heroes, who have mostly failed in one way or another, and prefer to look on at life as ironic spectators.

Frank Harris's most brilliant achievement is the paradoxical but convincing demonstration of how much there is of Hamlet in Macbeth; how again and again this blood-thirsty and barbarian chieftain of a savage age throws off his murderer's mask to reveal a visage pale with thought like Hamlet's; how he will often, stopping in the midst of headlong action, indulge in the most untimely soliloquies, and utter in the very accent and intonation of Hamlet's voice great generalisations on old age and death and sleep, telling us 'There's nothing serious in mortality,' or pausing, in the very crisis of his fate, to describe life as a walking shadow, and poor player on the stage.

Hamlet, it has been said, metaphysicalises the things he doesn't do, Macbeth the things he does; and it is no wonder that the practical Lady Macbeth despises him for his brain-sick thinking, so out of place in the drama and in the age they live in, and crying, 'give me the daggers!' goes off (after, however, permitting herself a pun like one of Hamlet's) to smear the grooms with blood.

III

What, then, are the ways of thought and feeling by means of which Shakespeare portrays himself (if we agree that he did portray himself) in Hamlet? One most important characteristic was noted by Coleridge, an aversion to personal and individual concerns, and a continual escape into generalisations and general reasonings. Hamlet is unable to resist any appeal to a general idea: 'Ay, Madam, it is common,' he assents to the Queen's truism in almost the first words he speaks; and on the platform a little later the sound of cannon sends him off into a philosophic temperance-speech which seems to make him forget that he is waiting to see his father's ghost.

Indeed, Hamlet seems to have infected almost all the characters in the play in which he figures—the King, the Queen, Polonius, and the Grave-digger—with this habit of his mind; and even the Ghost cannot help lingering on to indulge in at least one general reflection.

The detachment from existence which would naturally result from this habit of philosophic meditation, this way of seeing things in relation to the stars and the general scheme of things, and half-dissolved as it were in thought, shows itself in Hamlet and the Hamlet-like characters of Shakespeare's plays, sometimes in a sense of humorous absurdity and an ironic charity which seems like weakness, sometimes in an 'incorrigible divine levity,' as Mr. Bernard Shaw has well expressed it. Or again, 'Man, proud man,' seen thus from a distance, appears to him as nothing more than an angry ape playing before the eye of heaven fantastic tricks which make the angels weep.

Such a philosophic contemplator of the world, to whom the universe seems infinite, and himself nothing, and whose mind dwells among the unseen essences of things, will often find a deep meaning in what is trivial, and a trifling one in the most profound; he will often express himself, like Hamlet, in melancholy musings, in subtleties of self-analysis, in freaks and twists of thought, in phrases of incomparable beauty and bitterness, and in ribaldries which shock his hearers. To him, as to Antony when he gazes on the sunset-clouds, or to Prospero when the revels he had evoked were ended, existence will often seem like an unsubstantial pageant, and ourselves as dreams.

In these two of the greatest passages he wrote—and Prospero's speech has been described as the finest passage in Shakespeare, if not in all the literature of the world—I find the expression of one aspect, and to me the most essential aspect, of Shakespeare's spirit. Best of all, I love those plays, *Hamlet*, *As You Like It*, and *The Tempest*, which, like the *Sonnets* with their shimmering moods, are silvery-tinted with this cast of thought. To dream, to meditate, to lose ourselves in thoughts beyond the reaches of our souls, to love the gay appearances of the world and know them as illusions—this temper of an ironic mind, of a happy, enjoying, and yet melancholy nature, expresses itself in a secret rhythm, a cadence, a delicate and dream-like music which is, for me, the loveliest poetry of the world.

And now that I have returned from the Sahara of

our age to the realm of Shakespeare's imagination, with its glooms and splendours, the storms that threaten to tear the world from its hinges, and scenes that break the heart, what most delights me is to have found, or to imagine that I have found, aloof from the manifestations of what he called his 'rough magic,' the disenchanted Prospero of this dukedom, the dreamy Prince of the world of his own meditation. And if, lingering too long to listen, spell-bound, to this voice, surely the most magical, the most musical of all voices, I too have lost my reason, it is not amid the shouting theorists that you shall find me, but babbling, among the imbecile adorers, my praise.

Appendix

BOOKS ON SHAKESPEARE

O N P. 41 I quoted a sentence about Brandes'
book on Shakespeare from *A Sketch of Recent
Shakespearean Investigation,* 1893-1923, by
C. H. Herford, 1923 (Blackie & Son). In this book
will be found a clear account of the state of Shakespeare
study, at that date, and the contributions which had
been made to it in the way of textual knowledge and
critical interpretation. Of earlier criticism there is Mr.
Nicol Smith's *Eighteenth Century Essays on Shakespeare,* and that early and isolated masterpiece of interpretation, Maurice Morgann's *Character of Falstaff.*
Of the writings of our romantic critics, Hazlitt's *Characters of Shakespeare's Plays* is full of an appreciative
gusto that makes it delightful to read; the little that
Charles Lamb has written about Shakespeare is of the
rarest value, and Coleridge—what is one to say of Coleridge? All that he has written about Shakespeare has
been recently collected and admirably edited in two
volumes by Mr. T. M. Raysor—*Coleridge's Shakespearean Criticism* (Harvard University Press, 1931);
it makes almost intolerable reading, being full of
twaddle and preaching and German metaphysics, with
here and there, however, marvellous interpretations,
and, above all, little, immense insights into the proc-

esses of artistic creation. Of more recent books I have read with profit Moulton's *Shakespeare as a Dramatic Artist* (Oxford Press), and MacCallum's *Shakespeare's Roman Plays* (Macmillan). The two best books that I know about the Sonnets—Beeching's edition of them, and Richard Simpson's *Philosophy of Shakespeare's Sonnets*—are, unfortunately, like so many good books about Shakespeare, out of print. Of separate essays on the subject I think the finest is James Russell Lowell's *Shakespeare Once More,* in the first volume of *Among My Books.* Then there are three essays in Pater's *Appreciations,* four in Dr. A. C. Bradley's *Oxford Lectures on Poetry* (Macmillan), and three in his *Miscellany* (Macmillan). Of great interest also is Robert Bridges's paper, *The Influence of the Audience on Shakespeare's Drama* (Oxford Press). Of earlier essays, Bagehot's 'Shakespeare—the Man' in the first volume of his *Literary Studies,* and Leslie Stephen's essay on the same subject in Vol. IV of his *Studies of a Biographer,* are of a great value. Mr. George Gordon's paper on 'Shakespeare's English,' in the *S.P.E. Tract No. XXIX* (Oxford Press), is a masterly treatment of a subject which is treated at greater length in Abbott's *Shakespearian Grammar* (Macmillan)—a book beyond all praise. In addition to Mr. Mackail's recent *Approach to Shakespeare* (Oxford Press), two papers of the highest quality will be found in his *Lectures on Poetry* (Longmans), another in his *Studies of English Poets* (Longmans), and another, *Shakespeare After Three Hundred*

Years, printed separately among the annual Shakespeare Lectures of the British Academy. Of this admirable series (Oxford Press), I have profited in especial by *From Henry V to Hamlet* of Mr. Granville-Barker, the *Principles of Emendation in Shakespeare* of Mr. W. W. Greg, the *Elizabethan Shakespeare* of Mr. J. Dover Wilson, *A Plea for the Liberty of Interpreting* of Mr. Lascelles Abercrombie, *Shakespeare's Iterative Imagery* of Dr. Spurgeon, and the *Disintegration of Shakespeare* by Sir Edmund Chambers. The *William Shakespeare* (Oxford Press) of this great scholar is indispensable for special students; his *Shakespeare: A Survey* (Oxford Press) is an admirable handbook for the general reader, and I know of no better general introduction to the subject than his article on Shakespeare in the *Encyclopædia Britannica.* That monstrous volume, *A Book of Homage to Shakespeare* (Oxford Press), which contains, like the works of Shakespeare, a good deal of 'sad stuff,' contains also many essays of great interest, and it is a pity—since this book is out of print—that these are practically inaccessible to Shakespeare students. The publications of the great American scholar and most original critic, Professor E. E. Stoll, I mention on p. 25. Two recently published books should also be mentioned—Mr. Dover Wilson's *The Essential Shakespeare* (Macmillan), and an admirable interpretation of Shakespeare from a French point of view, M. Louis Gillet's *Shakespeare* (Paris, Grasset). Mr. F. G. Stokes's *Shakespeare Dictionary of Char-*

acters and Proper Names (Houghton Mifflin), Mr. C. T. Onions' *Shakespeare Glossary* (Oxford Press), and Schmidt's *Shakespeare Lexicon* (Stechert), are books of reference which every reader of Shakespeare should have at hand. My debt to the various scholars and critics I have mentioned, and above all to Dr. Bradley, Mr. Mackail, and Mr. Granville-Barker (whom I have found the most illuminating of them all), is beyond my computation, and I fear that I have too often enriched my essay with felicitous phrases from their writings.

Index